ZEITOUN TO TEMECULA
MY LIFE JOURNEY

Rami Mina

Dedication

To my wife, soul-mate, lover and friend, without whom I could not have had the good life. She is a cultured, refined and intelligent woman. She is my speed bump, my ballast, my sounding board, my counselor and my supporter. She puts up with my constant teasing and laughs at my boring, repeating jokes. I am lucky to share my life with her.

Contents

Introduction

By Bob Gibbons

The desire, maybe even the need, to write these paragraphs jumped into my mind when Rami sent me his manuscript to read – and I found it fascinating. But Rami knows me as a writer and so I figured he would be disappointed if I didn't step in and offer to write something. I offered to write a kind of Introduction – and Rami agreed – even though I'm not one of those people with a lofty title and great credibility who usually write these sorts of things.

My claim to fame (and the best job I ever had) is that for six or eight years, I was a ghostwriter. Back in the days when Kodak was the world leader in film for every purpose from theatrical movies to personal snapshots...when a 'Kodak Moment' meant a special time – and the 'yellow box' helped everyone remember their ordinary and extraordinary days...back in those days, I was the company's chief speechwriter for senior management. Those were the years of the nation's bicentennial and Kodak's own centennial – and there were lots of things to say, lots of audiences eager to listen, lots of speeches to be written – and so I did. Some of them turned out pretty well; others were just awful. I can no longer remember which were which. And it probably doesn't matter.

But I can remember the first time I met Rami. After my speechwriting (and other) years in Rochester, Kodak transferred me to the company's Hollywood Office where Rami was director of technology – and self-appointed leader of the welcoming party to celebrate the new people (including me) who would be working out of that storied location. There were three of us who came to Hollywood that year – and Rami threw a party in his home with a barbeque that was so big, so impressive, that many in the neighborhood thought his house was on fire.

Our regional manager was so impressed he asked Rami how he was able to pay for something so lavish. Rami explained he has simply "...sold some of our laboratory testing equipment we didn't need..." The manager was apoplectic. Rami actually "...*sold some Kodak equipment? To pay for a party?...*" Of course. That was Rami.

Because as I would come to know: When everyone was looking at something from one point of view, Rami saw it from quite another. Our first project together is one he covers in this book – helping Kodak to get an Academy Award – the company's eighth Oscar, more than any other company in the motion picture industry – for Scientific and Technical Achievement. Rami handled the facts and the presentation; I took care of adding some adverbs to the speeches, providing a bit of advice, and otherwise staying out of the way.

And it all went so well that our CEO was able to step in and take all the credit.

During my Kodak career, I had the great good fortune to work with the Walt Disney Company on several projects – and I get at least partial credit for the creation of 'Figment', the flying purple dragon from Kodak's 'Journey Into Imagination' pavilion at EPCOT. Figment represents the magical side of imagination, the child-like sense of wonder, the endless sense of curiosity, the eagerness to look for answers not in the back of the book, but in the shadows, under the bed, in places where no one else is looking – or even dares to look.

In our time together, I came to realize: there were at least two Figments in my life. One was a dragon; the other was Rami. And Rami may well have been the more amazing of the two.

Here was someone trained as an engineer, a scientist, somebody who learned that the world is governed by rational principles...but someone in whom the 'training' didn't quite 'stick'. All that education went in...but the imagination kept leaking out.

Like the lead character in one of my favorite movies, 'Big', Rami was the person willing to stand up in the middle of a management meeting and say, "I don't get it."

He was the one unafraid to ask: "Why are we doing this?" He was the one most likely – often *the only one* -- to express the 'minority opinion', even when that opinion was the only one to make any sense.

Whatever he did back then, whatever he does now, he does with enthusiasm, with a wide-eyed sense of wonder, with a real feeling of excitement not only for what's happening, but also for *what's possible*. When he called to tell me he had transitioned from a life of business and science and technology...and that he and Barbara were now living on a mountain where he was growing avocados, my only response was: *"But, of course..."*

That's Rami. You will get a real sense of the real person – and more -- in the story you are about to read because Rami's life bridges some interesting boundaries; he grew up in a country – and spent much of his career in a company – that have both changed nearly beyond recognition. What he learned along the way is not only fascinating it's also a bit instructive.

And endlessly entertaining because Rami is one of those people who always talks to you as an old friend – and writes the same way.
You are in for an adventure. Enjoy.

Bob Gibbons
Director of Marketing and Communications
(Retired)
Eastman Kodak Company

Preface

A few months ago, a close friend suggested I write my memoirs. The idea was totally foreign to me because I am not a writer. However, the more I thought about it, the more appealing it became. It's one of the more egotistical projects a person can undertake, but it does provide an opportunity to sum up the few years I've spent on earth in my own words.

I believe everything you read or anyone you meet, regardless how fleeting, has an effect on your life. So, I'm writing this for several reasons.

First and foremost is that by documenting many of my experiences, you will begin to understand the factors that made me the man I became. Maybe you will relate to something that will trigger you to become a better person.

The second is to shed some light on the culture existing in Egypt at the time I was growing up and the many changes that happened there, especially its transition from a stable monarchy to a democratic republic and the resulting social and economic upheaval.

The third reason is to document the many changes that occurred in the corporate world and how certain events resulted in profound changes to our family's circumstances.

The last reason is a selfish one. It is fun to remember and reminisce about my past and reflect on the various effects these experiences had on me. Hopefully, I will also be able to understand myself better and continue on the road of constant improvement.

Enough of the sappy sentiments.

Family History

I was born and brought up in Zeitoun (which means olive in Arabic and named for its many olive groves), one of Cairo's suburbs. Most of my father's family lived in Assiut, a small village in Upper Egypt (actually a couple of hundred miles south of Cairo, but called Upper Egypt because of its higher elevation.) My mother's family also originated in Assiut, but the majority of them moved to Cairo before I was born.

My paternal grandfather was a pharmacist. He and my grandmother had a girl, Camilla, followed by six boys who were named after famous people. Ernest (after Ernest Augustus, king of Hanover) was a pharmacist; Tugo (after the Japanese emperor) became curator of the Coptic Museum in Cairo. Emile (after the German chemist, Emil Fischer) was also a pharmacist, as was his brother William (the Conqueror). Next came my dad, Ramses (the Pharaoh, Ramses II) who was an electrical engineer and finally Samuel (biblical leader of Israel) who was an insurance salesman.

On my mother's side, my grandfather was an imposing railroad engineer. He and my grandmother had a big family: Emily (born when my grandmother was less than 15 years old), Cornelius, John, Zachariah, Soraya, my mother Mary, Neimat and Samuel. The boys all became doctors, engineers or lawyers and the girls completed at least two years of college, although all were stay-at-home moms. The fact that all my uncles and aunts were professionals only reflects the custom that all middle class Egyptians completed college and to do otherwise was a family disgrace.

Grandparents having afternoon tea with three of their children in their Zeitoun garden. Left to right: Neimat, Grandfather Matta Boctor, Grandmother Yasmine, Mother Mary and Samuel. Circa 1928

We visited our many cousins often during the school year and spent our entire summers together. We were as close to our cousins as most Americans are to their siblings.

There were five children in my immediate family, three boys and two girls. I was the oldest. Three years after I was born, my mother had three more children in quick succession. Samia, Karmy and Mona are separated by a year each. My youngest brother Sam was born five years later. He was a special needs child and required much of my parent's attention. Once the siblings came along, I felt that I received very little attention from my parents. That did not matter however, because I was the privileged first-born and was given the usual oldest son attention, indoctrination and consideration. My mother was very busy with the "group of three" and Sam. My father was usually at work or out of town on business trips, so I felt that I had to fend for myself. If unsure of a course of action, I took my best guess, proceeded and dealt with the consequences later. This helped me develop independence at an early age and defined my approach to new situations well into old age.

Mother and me and two of our servants

We lived in the pleasant neighborhood of Zeitoun in the same house from the time my parents got married until I was 16 years old and we immigrated to America. Our house was one of 12 identical villas in a compound surrounding a center mall with many fruit trees. Our neighbors also lived there for their entire lives. In fact my wife, children and I visited Egypt 30 years after we left and my friend Nagy's mother was still living in villa six. We lived in villa five and Uncle John, Auntie Sofie, Waguih and Hoda lived in villa four.

The villas were quite small, approximately 1000 square feet, with two bedrooms and a bathroom upstairs and a living room, dining room, kitchen and powder room downstairs. There was also a large veranda upstairs where we used to visit with friends and relatives on warm spring evenings. Each villa had a garden, driveway and a small servants' building in the back with its own running water and separate toilet.

A Muslim man lived with his two wives and their many children in villa eight. Although Muslims are allowed to have more than one wife, it was highly unusual among middle class Egyptians. As you would expect, the wives fought constantly but every week they piled into their little Czechoslovakian-made Skoda automobile for "Friday rides".

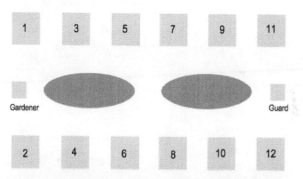

Our house was #5 and Uncle John's was # 4. My friend's villas were: Ingo #1, Nini #2, Nagi #6, Serague #10 and Haman #12

The mall between the houses was not paved and served as our playground where we rode bikes and played marbles and soccer with homemade tennis-sized balls made out of socks. We also spent hours building sophisticated cars, trucks and airplanes using

French-imported "Mekano" erector sets, or strung cans between our houses to play telephone.

As we grew older, we built crystal radio sets and collected and traded stamps. My favorite stamps were from Hungary because they had unique shapes, Madagascar and South Africa because they featured neat wild animals and Switzerland for their colored pictures and scenery. I longed to see the countries from which the stamps originated and this may have been the basis for my lifelong interest in travel and adventure.

Hungary

Top, Madagascar; Middle, South Africa; Bottom, Switzerland

Our bikes were essentially our identities. We spent many hours customizing, fixing and polishing them. On my tenth birthday, my parents surprised me with a brand new Phillips bike. It was a single speed, rod-braked (vs. more modern cable-braked), 28-inch black beauty. It was a little too high for me because my Dad wanted to make sure I did not outgrow it. We built wooden blocks to screw into the pedals and I rode it everywhere. That day, I was the "happiest boy in the world."

My pride & joy

As we reached puberty, we concentrated more on our schoolwork and girls. My favorite activity was getting together with my friends for a few hours before dinner and homework. On my way home from school, I pretended to be a banana or fig vendor and called the fruits out loud "testing" my changing voice. The whole neighborhood knew that I was home.

Ingo Leubner was my closest friend at that time. His family was German and I think his father worked at the German Embassy. Ingo had two older sisters. They sometimes called him to dinner from their upstairs window with their bras showing - how exciting!! He taught me some German and we spent so many hours together that we made our own pig-Latin-like language and practiced it to perfection. We wanted to have our own language so no one could understand us if it became necessary. It was simple yet effective when spoken quickly and fluently. "I can see you" would be "Ifificafanseefeeyoufou" and so on. Many years later, while working at the Kodak Research Labs, I met a German scientist named Ingo Leubner. He was the same age as my friend, looked like him and he too had two older sisters but unfortunately that is where the similarities ended.

Our schoolwork in seventh and eighth grade was quite rigorous. I usually started my homework right after supper and hardly ever finished before midnight without taking a break.

Nini was my first love and she lived in Villa 2. I was so excited every time I saw her that I got completely flustered and tongue-tied but somehow she got the message and became my girlfriend. We used to do our homework by a window where we could see each other and it was nice but tough to concentrate. We never kissed but just holding her hand and looking in her eyes was electrifying.

Early Childhood

My earliest childhood memories were of going to my maternal grandfather's house in Zeitoun for Sunday dinner. The house had an outbuilding with a dirt floor. It contained several large vats for pickles, olives and mish (rotting pungent cheese with worms). These vats as well as other staples were crammed in with two staid red and black classic sedans belonging to Uncle Samuel and Uncle Cornelius. The cars were driven a few years earlier while my uncles attended medical school and since then, to my knowledge, no one drove them. When I got a little older, I discovered that no one was allowed to own black and red cars because those were exclusively the king's colors. My uncles probably bought these cars before that law went into effect and could not drive them without getting into trouble.

Uncle Daki (short for Zachariah) was the most flamboyant of the brothers. He was a lawyer who wore white buck shoes and had a beautiful wife, Auntie Isis. They arrived for Sunday dinner in their bright yellow and red Buick convertible with a rumble seat. It was a treat to ride in that rumble seat.

Buick Similar to Uncle Daki's

I was the firstborn in my generation and the custom was for others to refer to my parents as "Abu" (Father of) Rami and "Om" (Mother of) Rami, so my name was bandied about freely. I was the center of the family's attention for three years until my sister and several cousins were born. Samia, Doreen, Shereef, Lina and Waguih were born in the same time frame. The next wave of cousins arrived shortly after and our family's adult attention was divided among my more than twenty cousins, whereas I had received my uncle's and aunt's attention exclusively. I believe all that attention contributed to my feelings of well-being and self-confidence.

Sham El Neseem (the smell of clover) festival stood out as an annual event. It signaled the beginning of spring and was typically celebrated by going on a picnic and eating green onions, smelly sardines and hard-boiled eggs. We woke up early in the morning, got dressed in fancy clothes and walked to my grandparents' house for the picnic in their large yard. My father gave me a few coins and we stopped on the way to buy some firecrackers. The firecrackers were small marble-sized paper spheres wrapped around a little explosive material and held together with a thin black wire. We exploded these little bombs by throwing them hard against a solid surface. Small bomb explosions could be heard throughout the day, wherever you went.

When I was about five years old, my grandfather retired from the railroad, sold his house in Zeitoun and built an eighteen-apartment resort house in Alexandria, a few feet from the Mediterranean. He gave each of his children an apartment large enough to accommodate their families and rented the remaining ones to the public for income. Each year, as soon as school was out, we would caravan from our respective cities, Cairo or Assiut, to Alexandria to spend the summer together.

These were among the most pleasant times of the year. We spent every day on the beach, getting sunburned initially, but tanning to deep brown "natives" by the end of the summer. We spent our days swimming, boating or fishing off the rocks. If it was a red or black flag (rough sea) day, I went fishing using my bamboo fishing pole with a bent straight pin for a hook and a cork for a bobber. I caught tiny shrimp in the tide pools to use as bait. I generally fished by myself all day and brought home a bucket of tiny fish similar in size to smelt or sardines. One of the servants gutted, cleaned and fried them and we ate them for dinner, bones and all. They were delicious.

We spent the afternoons making and flying kites, playing chess or cards or being entertained by the many street performers who came to our building. There were magicians, a pied piper playing bagpipes, who we called "the headache man", puppeteers and vendors who sold roasted corn on the cob, nuts, ice cream and other snacks.

In the evenings all of us (adults and children) went for long walks on the plage (board-walk), talking, buying and eating roasted corn from street vendors, telling jokes and enjoying the evening sea breezes. Once home, we had a light snack and went to bed.

My grandfather's desk was huge and had a built-in bookshelf in the front, which contained a nicely bound set of Encyclopedia Britannica. I spent many hours sitting in front of his desk on the floor immersed in all kinds of interesting topics from oceanography to zoology.

Most meals were eaten at my grandparents' apartment and cooked by Shafeek, their long-time cook, and enjoyed with all my cousins. Nothing compared to my grandmother's (really Shafeek's) Greek chicken noodle soup (Avgolemono).

After the day's main meal, usually eaten about two o'clock, my grandmother and aunts migrated to the hall where they talked and had afternoon tea and cookies (also served by Shafeek). My grandfather usually took an afternoon nap and we, the children, started our afternoon fun.

Our fathers usually worked in Cairo during the week and joined us on weekends. We anxiously waited for their arrival on Friday afternoons, partially because we missed them but more importantly, because they usually brought us small gifts. We spent our waiting time counting different colored cars or betting on their arrival time. Weekend after dinner routines were a little different. After the main meal, the women retired to the hall as usual and the men joined my grandfather in the living room where they had loud heated discussions about religion and/or politics.

The long fun-filled summer days spent with my extended family probably influenced my comfort with people and contributed to my outgoing personality and the proximity to the Mediterranean reinforced my love for all things aquatic.

Memories of my early childhood are fragmented at best, so I won't attempt to make them into a coherent story. Here are a few of those disjointed memories:

- I clearly recall the Palestinian/Israeli war. Our windows were painted deep blue to prevent any light from being seen from enemy aircraft. When the air raid sirens sounded, we turned off all the lights then heard airplanes, followed by loud explosions. It was scary because I thought all our villas would be bombed out. That war ended the existence of Palestine and the emergence of the Israeli nation.

- Dad, who was an electrical engineer at the government telephone unit, left for work about 9:00 am and returned about 2:00 pm. It was the custom for men to wear a red Fez with black tassel, called a TARBOUSH. He kept it on a small console table next to the front door when he was home. As soon as he returned from work, we had our main meal for the day after which my parents retired for a 1-2 hour nap. After the nap we freshened up, had a light sandwich and went out to socialize. We visited relatives at their houses or met friends at one of the sporting clubs, where the adults talked and the children played. At other times we went for walks and the smell of jasmine in the spring was almost intoxicating. We returned home about 9:00 pm, totally exhausted and glad to hop into bed. On the way home, I

sometimes commented that I was so tired I wasn't
sure I could make it up the stairs to my bedroom.
This routine was usually repeated six times a
week.

- My father's mother and some uncles and aunts on
both sides lived in Assiut, a village about 200
miles south of Cairo. We went there once a year
by train. My father and brothers generally stayed
with his mother Taita Fatan, who traditionally
wore a long black dress and a black headscarf. My
mother and sisters usually stayed with her sister
Auntie Emily, who was married to Dr. Faheem,
an eye surgeon. They had a large family of 12
kids, most of who graduated from medical school.
Instead of a car, they owned a horse drawn
carriage, so about 20 minutes before we went out
they called down to their livery to harness and
prepare the horses. I loved sitting high up beside
the driver. I usually stayed with my Aunt Camilla
because I was her favorite. Her two sons, Maher,
Mokhtar and I liked hunting for mourning doves
with BB rifles. We sometimes brought home a
dozen or more. The servants cleaned and roasted
them and we had them for dinner. They tasted
like tender squabs and were delicious especially
because we hunted them. Our ancestors must
have experienced great joy hunting and gathering
their food. Regardless of where everyone stayed,

we always met for dinner and usually got together for our daily activities.

- As my father was promoted, he became qualified to use one of the government's railroad cars for an extended vacation. We went to Upper Egypt, specifically Luxor & Aswan, to learn ancient history. The destination was not quite as interesting as the trip to get there. That railroad Pullman car was the epitome of luxury. It included three bedrooms, a dining room, a living room, a kitchen and a full staff including a cook, chambermaid and steward. My father arranged with our destination's conductor for coupling and decoupling from the scheduled service and the Pullman car was left on a track in the railroad yard of our destination city. Naturally, there were no platforms and the cars were extremely high, so we used a high ladder for entry and exit. My parents and the cook made the daily menu and all meals were freshly prepared. Unfortunately my most vivid memory of that trip was my father drilling me on the multiplication table. I had trouble with 6x7 and he mercilessly twisted my ear until I got it consistently correct. To this day, my ears are more than a little asymmetric and contribute to my unique appearance.

Egypt of My Childhood

Egyptians could be divided into three classes. The first class super rich comprised about 3% of the population and were the Pashas (relatives of the king) and owned most of the agricultural land and industries. The second class professionals comprised about 20% of the population and enjoyed a lifestyle very similar to that of Western Europe and the United States. Most were college graduates and lived in cities that were modern and clean, very unlike today's Cairo and other third world country cities. The remainder of the population was the third class peasants (fellaheen). They worked as farmhands, servants to the middle class and super rich or in other menial jobs. They primarily lived in mud huts along with their domesticated animals in villages with unpaved streets. Egypt was essentially two separate countries – City Egypt and Village Egypt

The three classes lived separately but all were happy and accepted their positions. We were in the middle class and had no interaction with the super rich and very little interaction with the lower class except for our servants. Most middle class families had at least one servant. If they were lucky, they acquired a servant about the age of 12 when their kids were born and that servant would remain with the family for the rest of his/her life. Sometimes servants elected to return to their villages to get married and start their own families. This disrupted the family because they had to go through the difficult process of finding a replacement. Neighbors and friends generally recommended relatives of their own servants. The limited number of available individuals in the right age group generally narrowed the field.

We had a succession of servants, some men, some women, some old and some young. Our longest serving individual was Rhoda. Her parents brought her to our house when she was about eleven. I must have been about the same age. My parents negotiated with her parents on her pay, which was about five Egyptian pounds per month. Her parents came to collect her pay each month. As soon as Rhoda arrived, my mother cut her hair and de-liced her head by washing it with kerosene. After her bath, she put on a brand new floral dress, which my mom made, and wore it with pride. Within a short time, Rhoda was transformed from a dirty village girl into a clean fresh city girl and adapted well into our family routines. Rhoda slept in the servant's quarters, a one room building in the back of our house, which contained its own toilet and sink.

Servants generally ate in the kitchen after we finished our meals. They used different silverware and plates and even used separate bathrooms. Once the work was done, which was rare, they had a chance to relax, play and talk with our neighbor's servants. I often heard them laugh and joke so I assumed they were not depressed because they were less privileged as their city life was better than their village life.

My mom always needed one or more full time servants because housework was labor intensive. Although she was a stay-at-home mom, she had five children and everything had to be done manually. Once we left for school, my mother sent the servant to the grocery store, vegetable store and butcher to buy the day's raw food. Nothing was canned or frozen. Even milk was unpasteurized and we had to heat it to the point where the cream rose to the top to kill any bacteria that may be present. My mom skimmed the heavy cream and used it to make delicious cream and jelly or cream and olive sandwiches. If we were having chicken, we bought a live chicken. The servant slit its throat and it flopped around until its blood was drained. My mother and the maid then plucked the feathers, dressed it and put it in a pot of boiling water. Once parboiled, they prepared it into the desired recipe. All vegetables were raw and had to be prepped. It literally took my mom and the servant all day to clean house, shop, and prepare the main meal. My mother constantly shouted at the maids and complained that they were more trouble than they're worth. This was atypical for her because she was generally gentle and peaceful. It must have been the thing to do because I noticed that most of our neighbors and relatives complained about their maid's inadequacies.

All public transportation such as buses, trains and metros were divided into three classes. First class was in the front and had a few plush cushioned seats. The second class came next and was adequate and comfortable. The third class was in the back and had wooden, backless benches all crowded together.

The separation of classes was complete. The fellaheen listened to different music, shopped in different stores and wore different clothes. Elementary education was compulsory but the masses attended public schools and the middle class attended either English or French private schools. There was never a crossover from one class to the other.

In or around 1952, the masses or fellaheen became dissatisfied with the inequities and this precipitated the 1952 revolution. Fires were set all over Cairo. Mr. Neal Wilson, an American missionary and founder of Egypt's Seventh Day Adventist Church was driving home when a mob saw him, pursued him, doused his car with gasoline and tried to set it on fire. The crowd could see he was a foreigner and they associated foreigners with the oppressive British who backed King Farouk. He escaped by driving on the sidewalk around barricades, mowed down some pedestrians and eventually got away.

King Farouk (the English puppet) was ousted shortly after the short revolution and army officer Gamal Abd El Nasser assumed power. Nasser's regime fundamentally changed the existing equilibrium and plunged Egypt into its existing chaotic state but he became the common man's hero.

Nasser nationalized most private companies, confiscated large land parcels and financial holdings from the rich and divided the land among the poor. He also made college education completely free.

These changes were designed to help the masses but the opposite happened. The peasants, who previously were supported by their bosses, now became landowners. Each received an acre or so but they could not support themselves on that. Colleges produced many graduates but there were not enough jobs to absorb them. The government then required the recently nationalized businesses to hire their quota of graduates whether they needed them or not. Productivity plummeted and salaries were reduced. Thousands of dissatisfied idle college graduates occupied space in factories and offices, could not earn a living wage and were forced to live with their parents.

About that time, Christians were increasingly discriminated against and the government eventually decreed that all government deputy generals must be of the Muslim faith. My father, who had achieved that rank, was demoted and many of his junior engineers leap-frogged over him and became his supervisors. This eventually caused my father's resignation from the government and planted the seed of emigration from our beloved country.

A few years after the revolution, Nasser nationalized the Suez Canal. Now duties levied on crossing ships would go to Egypt instead of England and France. This precipitated the short Suez Canal war. Again we painted our windows blue, turned the lights off when the sirens were activated and heard the loud French Mirages, Russian Migs, and British jets bomb our houses. We often found shrapnel in our yard. On one occasion I was standing inside our local bicycle shop during a daytime air raid and happened to see red-hot shrapnel coming at me from the corner of my eye. I ducked just in time because it missed me and lodged in the wall behind me!

Peace was negotiated a few days after the war started and a large number of UN peacekeeping troops descended on Egypt. It was fun to see them in their varied uniforms, hear them talk in different languages and learn about their cultures.

Education and Religion

Education and religion are generally the two important factors affecting most people. Our religion became a way of life and had a significant effect on essentially every aspect of my existence well into adulthood.

Most Egyptian Christians are members of the Coptic Church. It is a religion very similar to Greek and Russian Orthodox. Their papal leader is believed to be a direct descendent of St. Mark, as opposed to the Roman Catholic pope who is a descendent of St. Peter. My parents converted from Coptic Christians to Seventh Day Adventists (SDA) about the time I started Kindergarten. Some may think that is an unusual change for Egyptians and it was. In fact, no one in our family ever contemplated leaving the centuries-entrenched Coptic religion for any other faith. It happened because my dad became very interested in how history correlated with the Bible. While he and his brother, Uncle Tugo the museum curator, researched the topic, an advertisement in the local newspaper attracted their attention. An American SDA evangelist, Mr. Neal Wilson was going to address that very same topic in an upcoming series of lectures. My father and his brother made arrangements to attend. After the sermon, they talked to Mr. Wilson well into the night and my father continued to attend more of Mr. Wilson's meetings.

It didn't take long for my parents to "get hooked". Not only that, they succeeded in convincing several of my uncles and aunts to join them in becoming SDAs. This caused a lot of consternation with my maternal grandfather and became the source of many spirited debates.

The fact that I was essentially five years old at the time this change occurred was significant because I had had five years of "normal" up-bringing before the Adventists religion infiltrated our lives. My siblings were not so lucky and I believe that had a profound effect on their ability to deal with "normal worldly people".

The SDAs believe the bible literally. The holy day was the seventh day of the week, Saturday, the Sabbath. It started at sundown Friday night and continued for 24 hours until sundown Saturday. They believe they are "in this world but not of this world". This principle alone excluded us from participating in many normal activities. Attending motion picture theaters and bowling alleys was forbidden, although we could see "clean movies" at church socials or other venues limited to SDAs. We believed that our bodies are temples of Christ and were not allowed to defile them by ingesting anything that could harm them. The bible specifically excludes eating sea creatures without fins and scales (shell fish, shrimp, lobster, eel, shark...etc) or any animal that does not chew its cud (ruminant) <u>and</u> without a cloven hoof (pig, rabbit, horse...etc). Although not specifically mentioned, eating meat of any kind (beef, foul or fish) was frowned upon because of its propensity to spread disease and/or cause cancer. My mother made a meat substitute called gluten by kneading dough under the faucet until all the starch was washed away and it became rubbery like real meat. It tasted terrible, as did the non-meat hotdogs made from it. Of course tobacco, alcohol and caffeine were strictly forbidden. Even hot chocolate contained some caffeine so our hot drink of choice was Postum, which was made from molasses, cornmeal and wheat germ and it tasted as bad as one would expect. YUK!!

As a result of this religious conversion, my parents interacted with many American missionaries and decided to place me in an English rather than a French school. English is a more universal language and the fact that there was a good English school within walking distance of our house cemented that decision.

I started Kindergarten at the age of five at the English Mission College (EMC). It was an Anglican but not too religious school.   My teacher, Miss Shenouda was a short, black-haired lady with a stern disposition.   Although she was tough, she liked me and this made my first year at school a little bit less daunting. Like Kindergarten teachers everywhere, she wrote the alphabet on the blackboard and started teaching us the sounds each letter makes. I remember making the sounds to my mother or servant as they walked me to and from school.

Most of my elementary school classes had about thirty kids and all of us had to wear uniforms. It was brown shorts with a bib (barbatose), white shirt and socks and brown oxford shoes. Here again, memory is fading, so I will try to insert a few memories without any specific order:

- My friends constantly teased me about my asymmetric ears.   They may have been more pronounced when my head was smaller.

- We had to lay our heads on the desk for an afternoon nap. One afternoon I happened to look up and saw our teacher, Miss Gohary, lifting up her skirt to show her new American girdle to one of her fellow teachers.   It was an embarrassing moment for both of us.

- We had big black desks with an inkwell but were only allowed to write with pencils. It was a 'red letter day' when our penmanship improved to the point where we could use a pen for writing (never a ballpoint).   We wrote with real pens with exchangeable nibs that had to be dipped in the inkwell. Fountain pens came later and became an item to covet.

- I always walked to school and our path passed by the king's palace in El Kobbah. I peeked through the big gates at the beautiful gardens. Whenever the king travelled, traffic was stopped and soldiers lined both sides of the street every ten feet. The king drove by in one of his many red and black limousines.

- Many times a month I saw herds of camels, usually four to eight, being led to the slaughter house which was not too far from our house. I don't know if they were slaughtered for their hides or meat or both.

My sequential memories started about the age of ten. As I thought back about my life for writing these memoirs, I figured out that my father resigned from government service about the time I was that age. Fortuitously, the Seventh Day Adventist Church had just purchased a small guava grove in Gabal-El-Asfar, a neighboring town, and hired my father to develop and build a high school work/study farm for the many orphanage boys scattered in the villages.

I believe that part of my father's package for accepting this job was free tuition for my siblings and me in the local SDA primary school. I transferred from the English Mission College to the SDA School in fifth grade. There, we did not have to wear uniforms, the classes were smaller, less structured and several of the classes were combined grades.

I loved my fifth grade teacher, Miss Mary. She came to our house for dinner one afternoon and I was so enamored with her that when she bent down to tie her shoes, I gathered enough nerve and kissed her on the cheek. She smiled, said "Oh! Thank you" and gave me a big hug. I was in seventh heaven the rest of that day. I guess I was precociously forward.

By the eighth grade, the classes were quite small. I was valedictorian of my class, but alas, I was first out of only three!

One of my grade school classes

Although the picture above shows a regular albeit small class size, it included several stand-ins. The lady sitting in the back corner was our teacher's wife and also one of our teachers.

I had several embarrassing moments at the SDA School, the worst of which was when I wet my pants in fifth grade. I guess the teacher was so interesting that I didn't raise my hand to go to the bathroom until it was too late. Needless to say my classmates mercilessly teased me until I transferred out of that school three years later. On another occasion, I ripped my pants in the playground, covered my butt with my book bag and went home to change.

One afternoon, I had a severe headache in school and the incessant Muslim prayer chants blasting from the surrounding minarets exacerbated the pain. I really didn't want to walk home and being totally devout, I fervently prayed that God would transport me home. Occasionally, as I walked home, my Uncle Edward drove by and offered me a ride. This day, I started walking and reached a point where I had to make a decision. Should I take the long road and increase the chances that my uncle would see me or take a short cut through the fields and get home faster? I decided to take the shortcut. To my surprise, the neighborhood soda pop vendor came along on his bike and offered me a ride home. This was the first and only time that ever happened and it went a long way in affirming my faith.

As mentioned earlier, my seventh and eighth grade years were busy with lots of homework and other activities. It was not unusual to start my homework as soon as I got home from school and not finish until midnight. I remember having to memorize all of the U.S. states and their capitals on one night. I then had to complete my math and English homework.

One time I sneaked into our teacher's desk after everyone went home and discovered her math book (teacher's edition). My heart beat a little faster as I peaked inside and there, right in front of me, were the answers to all our math problems for the rest of the year. You know the rest of the story: yes, I used her answer book frequently. It was later discovered that some kids cheated on their spelling tests. The teacher, the one sitting in the corner of the picture above, gave us a stern lecture and stated that we should all be ashamed of ourselves. Fortunately I was not involved in THAT one. She went on to say that I, Rami, was the only one who did not cheat and they should all follow my example. It's true I did not cheat on the spelling test, but I did copy the math answers, so you can imagine the guilt I felt. I didn't do anything about it until many years later after we immigrated to America, when the guilt about this incident became unbearable. I finally sent her a letter admitting my transgression and asked for forgiveness. I did not receive a reply but a few months later my sister received a letter from that teacher telling her she was forgiven and that she was very proud of her for clearing her conscience. I didn't care that she confused me with my sister because my guilt was finally lifted.

The summer after sixth grade, my Dad and I left Alexandria and the rest of my family to attend a religious camp meeting in the Gabal-El-Asfar. We slept in tents and the area was infested with scorpions that got into our tents and found their way to our shoes. We carefully inspected our shoes before putting them on and fortunately none of us were bitten. I took my brand new shaving kit to the stream to shave with the men (even though I had nothing to shave). I was extremely proud to be considered old enough to go with them.

At one of the morning sessions, the minister asked if there was anyone in the audience who wanted to be baptized into the SDA church. The Adventists baptize by immersion at the age of twelve so that any prospective member would fully understand this life altering commitment. I raised my hand without hesitation and without asking my father. After a few lessons, I became baptized into the SDA church.

As mentioned earlier, the SDA religion infiltrated every aspect of our lives and was all encompassing as illustrated by our weekly routine. We usually woke up early Saturday (Sabbath) morning to go to church. Church started with a hymn service at 9:30 and was followed by Sabbath school, which was broken down by age groups to study and discuss the bible lesson in an informal atmosphere. We reunited for the main church service at 11:00 that consisted of a sermon preached by one of the missionaries in English and translated to Arabic by one of the bilingual members. My father was frequently one of the translators.

We generally invited a few church members to join us for dinner (late lunch). Our next service, vespers, came just before sundown. We prayed again, sang a few hymns and listened to another short sermon. After vespers and sundown, we attended a church social where we played ping-pong or chess with our friends, made and ate ice-cream and sometimes watched a pre-selected 16 mm movie like Snow White or the Wizard of Oz.

These church activities were in addition to the usual Friday night vespers to usher in the Sabbath and a Wednesday night prayer meeting.

One would think that the schedule was sufficient to ensure total communication with our Lord but it wasn't. Every afternoon (other than church nights) my mother introduced the tradition of worship hour. It was a time when we had to stop whatever we were doing and meet with our parents to study a short bible lesson, sing a hymn and say our prayers. We generally invited whatever friends were around to join us.

I hated and was embarrassed by this ritual, because again, it separated us from the "mainstream". Now, as I look back, I see that our schedule was bordering on cult indoctrination. All this interaction with separatists caused us to believe that we were the chosen ones and anyone not like us was evil. It was a dangerous way to be in a "live and let live" world.

At that time, there were no SDA high schools nearby so I transferred back to the English Mission College (EMC). Starting in high school, the boys' and girls' schools became segregated. The girls' school, chapel and classes were on the North end of the campus and the boys' facilities on the South end. In effect there were three separate schools on one campus, the elementary school, the boys' high school and the girls' high school. Each school had its own yard, classes and chapel. Large gardens separated the schools and it was always fun to have outside classes on nice days, especially if the girls were outside also.

Unlike the American system where career choices are addressed in college, Egyptian students' career choices were determined by school performance. As early as the ninth grade, the students who did well in elementary school were assigned to a science curriculum and the rest to a business and commerce curriculum. In essence, we had no choice because no one who could qualify for the sciences would choose the less prestigious business classes, regardless of their interest. Most classes were common to all and we separated for our respective curricula for one or two periods a day.

Lower and upper four (ninth and tenth grade) were considered general secondary education years, lower and upper five (eleventh and twelfth grade) were more rigorous and focused on preparing us for the Baccalaureate examinations. These were of utmost importance because they determined your career path. The highest achieving students from our school were admitted to Oxford or Cambridge Universities to pursue a career of their choice. The rest were ranked with all other high school graduates throughout Egypt. The highest achieving students of this group were automatically admitted to the schools of engineering or medicine and the rest were allocated positions in other fields depending on their grade on that examination. In other words, a student's career path was determined by the results of that exam and not by their personal aptitude or interest.

One of the most anticipated results of the school year was our class ranking. In fact, that ranking carried more weight with our parents than our actual report card. Aunt Sofie always asked me how I ranked because her son Waguih generally came in first. I usually ranked third to seventh out of our total class of about forty, a respectable if not great position. It's interesting to note that the guy who consistently came in first throughout high school became a professional poker player in London and did very well.

Transferring back to the larger English Mission College (EMC) School was quite traumatic for me because I had just left a small school where I knew everyone and everyone knew me and was similar to me in terms of life experiences and beliefs. I was somewhat intimidated by my new, non-Adventist, fellow students who went to movies, listened to popular songs, ate meat and drank soda pop. In other words, they were normal and I was not. I felt I did not measure up.

As a defense mechanism, I immersed myself in schoolwork and became a quiet, studious nerd who joined the chess club and retreated into the background. To make matters worse, I was not athletic and shied away from joining basketball and soccer games. I did however, join thirty or more boys run in our annual cross-country race. We wore white shirts, shorts, shoes and socks and ran in fields, across steams and over meadows and I finished in the middle of the pack.

At home, I was a different person. I was outgoing, independent, friendly and somewhat naughty. Once, my father was away on a business trip and left our car in the garage, which was around the corner from our house. Although I was only fourteen years old, I thought I could sneak the car out, drive it to school and return it without being caught. I made it to school without incident and some of my schoolmates saw me driving which made me into an instant celebrity. Unfortunately on the way home, a policeman spotted me and thought I was too short and young to drive, so he stopped me. A crowd quickly gathered and to my surprise, our gardener materialized and bribed the policeman who let me go. I breathed a sigh of relief and quickly drove the car into the garage and walked in the house. The gardener showed up a moment later and relayed the whole incident to my mother who was not too happy or lenient with me.

1952 Opel Olympia identical to ours

Another time I decided to ride my bike to the Gabal-El-Asfar farm, a twenty-mile trip. The ride there and back took a lot longer than expected and my parents were quite worried when I did not show up for worship hour or dinner. I was punished for not getting permission before such an extended adventure.

On another occasion, my friends, Hamam, Ingo and I heard that cats could leap great distances and land on their feet unharmed. We decided to test the theory and threw three of our neighborhood cats out of windows from different heights. Sure enough, the theory is correct. They all landed on their feet unharmed.

The final example of my naughty behavior was the most dangerous. I read that mixing strong acids with metal produces hydrogen and it was lighter than air. I bought some acid from the local drugstore, put some in a coke bottle and added a piece of metal which I had cut from the back of our kitchen counter top. I put a balloon around the bottle's neck and sure enough, the balloon inflated. I tied the balloon and sent it floating up. I had great fun repeating the process and writing messages to whoever found them. I also discovered that hydrogen was explosive. One early evening I took one of the hydrogen filled balloons to a remote section of our yard to test the power of the explosion. I reasoned that the small amount of hydrogen was not sufficient to cause much harm, but just in case, I made sure no one was around. I held the hydrogen-filled balloon in my hands, looked the other way and ignited it. The resulting explosion singed the hair on my arms and was much greater than I anticipated. Needless to say I stayed away from that process from that point on. Ironically, I ended up as a chemist, frequently handling strong acids.

Every Monday morning, I put on my school uniform (brown pants, beige shirt, tan blazer and striped tie) and resumed my quiet, nerdy, studious demeanor. Just beneath that surface was the desire to emulate the more popular Peter Sykalli and Robbie Maronian. They were loud and made fun of our English teacher, Mr. Lynch. He was the typical absent-minded professor who wore non-matching socks. One time Peter or Robbie threw a piece of chalk at Mr. Lynch as he faced the blackboard. No one admitted to throwing it, so we were all punished by Saturday detention. We decided to come in wearing girls' clothes with scarves over our mouths and carrying toy guns. I don't recall the exact outcome, but I was happy to be included with the bad guys.

I ran into Robbie Maronian at Kodak's Photographic Technology division many years later. He happened to be working in the same building and floor as I was! It was quite a coincidence to find two Egyptian high school classmates working in the same division of the same company half a world away. I expected to see the same fun loving Robbie I knew in high school. Instead I found a reserved, serious man.

Our roles had completely reversed. I became more outgoing and he turned into a suspicious, withdrawn individual.

In or about my second year of high school, all schools were nationalized. The study of Arabic became compulsory, the Koran had to be read and studied by every student and this was enforced by frequent visits from stern government inspectors. Nationalization also dictated that schools had to be closed on Friday, the Islamic holy day. Schools were also closed on Sundays, the Christian holy day and that posed a problem for us Seventh Day Adventists. I didn't mind having three-day-weekends but I had to make special arrangements for Saturday classes and exams.

My dad understood that this was an unsustainable position once I started college. Also, my father's job at the SDA church was nearing completion and he needed to find another. The proverbial straw that broke the camel's back was the increasing discrimination felt by Christians in everyday life. These three factors precipitated our concerted effort to immigrate to the United States.

Immigration

In the late forties and early fifties, the Egyptian middle class was fairly comfortable. It was rare for anyone to want to leave Egypt for anything but a short vacation. My father, however, had enough foresight to realize that our situation warranted a move to America. The United States accepted a number of immigrants from each country known as a quota of immigrants. I'm not sure how many families were accepted each year from Egypt. I do know that my father placed our name on the list in 1948. Ten years later, as the factors affecting our desire to leave became more critical, our name was not even close to being considered for emigration.

Another way to obtain a visa was for an American company to request the US government to issue a visa on the basis that the individual's skills were needed and not available in this country. My dad reasoned that obtaining employment in an American firm was a more expeditious way to acquire a visa. Fortunately he was fairly well known in the telephone business, travelled the world presenting papers and had a large network of colleagues. He wrote over a hundred letters to friends and potential employers. Many invited him for interviews, which he could not accept because he was half a world away. Finally a small company in Chicago, Kellogg Switchboard and Supply Company offered him a job, sight unseen. They offered him $6000/year, a beginning engineer's salary. This was a win-win decision. We received our visa and they hired an experienced engineer for a starting engineer's salary.

My father received his employment offer in the spring of 1958 and we needed to start school in America the following fall. We filed immigration documents immediately and things moved very quickly. I applied to attend Broadview Academy, a Seventh Day Adventist boarding high school in La Fox, Illinois, about an hour's drive from Chicago.

For me, an adventurous 16 year-old, it was a very exciting time. I was interested in everything from booking our voyage, to applying to a new school, to wondering what the streets were going to be like. We heard of the German autobahn and the American freeways, where drivers could go faster than 100 kilometers per hour!! Now I was going to actually experience them. You can imagine how I felt trying to anticipate all the new experiences. It was a heady time for anyone, let alone excitable Rami.

We became celebrities with our friends and cousins because we were actually trailblazing to

America. The large influx of Egyptians immigrating to America was not until 1969, more than a decade later.

Many of my aunts and cousins poured over Sears and Roebuck and Montgomery Wards catalogues, endlessly circling items they wanted my mother to purchase in the States. My cousin Tawfik who had just finished his ENT residency in Chicago returned to Egypt the summer before we left and advised us on where to look for housing, the cost of living and many other useful details too numerous to document here.

At that time I was so interested in cars, I could identify any car made by as little as 10% of its identifying characteristics. In Egypt, most cars were at least a decade old but they were spotless and gleaming. Pride in ownership was obvious. The servants, or more often the night watchmen, spent their days washing and polishing their masters' vehicles. In fact, in Alexandria, where cars were exposed to the salt sea air, most cars' chrome surfaces were heavily shellacked to deter rust formation. It was very exciting to be going to a location where I could see, feel and touch the newest cars, essentially as they came off the assembly line.

The voyage itself was extremely interesting to me because I had never been on an airplane or ship. In fact, I had never been out of the country. We decided to travel by steamship instead of by airplane because the cost was significantly lower. The least expensive mode of sea transportation was a cargo vessel, so that is what we booked. We literally came to America on a "banana boat" (not exactly but close). I will discuss the crossing later.

As I mentioned earlier, we lived in our house in Zeitoun from the time I was born to the time we left Egypt. Early in my parent's marriage, my father was interested in carpentry and had opened a furniture shop as a side business. There, he built all the furniture our family needed. Our dining room set had an elaborate mahogany buffet, hutch, dining room table and eight chairs. My parents' bedroom set included a substantial teak cupboard, dresser and bed. He even built a large, glass-topped, ebony desk, which was placed in our large foyer. Our house was filled with great looking homemade furniture and elaborate Persian carpets. Unfortunately, my parents decided to sell everything and start fresh in America.

After school was out in June 1958, we sold the car and all the furniture. We terminated the lease on the Zeitoun villa, closed our local bank accounts and released the servants as the final documents were being processed. Before long, all the transition details were completed and we enjoyed our last summer in Alexandria with only the clothes on our back.

We made plans to board our ship in mid-September in Suez. Uncle John, Auntie Sofie,

Waguih and Hoda, as well as Uncle Samuel and Auntie Mimi drove us from Alexandria to Suez. At that time Uncle Samuel was a ranking government official in spite of his Christianity. He received preferential treatment because he was Nasser's personal physician. My uncle facilitated our boarding process and we left the country without any kind of customs inspections.

My first impression of our ship was different from my expectation. Instead of a rusty cargo ship, I found a freshly painted ship with clean, pleasant decks and an attentive staff. We were welcomed aboard with a large basket of fruit and champagne. Auntie Sofie marveled at the shiny red delicious apples, an expensive delicacy that is not generally available in our warm country.

The ship was of Greek registry, the officers were British and the crew was primarily American. Many cargo ships have a few staterooms to accommodate the owners on their world travels. Our ship had four spacious, well-appointed staterooms, each with its own bathroom. My parents and youngest brother Sam occupied one, my sisters the second, my brother and me the third and the fourth stateroom was occupied by two young Indian guys headed for postgraduate studies in America. We were treated like royalty by the officers and crew and enjoyed all meals at the captain's table.

We sailed from Suez, a port on the northern coast of the Red Sea, through the Suez Canal, across the Mediterranean Sea, past the Rock of Gibraltar, across the Atlantic and finally to NYC. The trip took approximately ten days.

The Suez Canal is a narrow sea level strip of salt water cut through the desert connecting the Red and Mediterranean Seas. Only one ship can pass at a time. There is a large salt-water lake halfway between the Mediterranean and Red Seas, where Northbound and Southbound vessels anchor to wait their turn to navigate the remainder of their crossings.

We crossed the canal in 1958, two years after it had been nationalized by Egypt. The new Egyptian pilots had gained enough navigating experience to successfully take ships across the narrow channel.

The Suez Canal was designed and built by the French architect, Ferdinand De Lesseps, who was later commissioned to build the Panama Canal. We had an occasion to cross the Panama Canal many years later and the two are as different as night and day. The Suez Canal is essentially a ditch dug though a dry FLAT barren sea level desert. It is about 112 miles long. The Panama Canal cuts through lush dense tropical vegetation between the Atlantic and Pacific oceans and traverses significantly hilly terrain.

De Lesseps initial efforts to build a sea level canal in Panama, similar to the Suez Canal, failed miserably. About 21,900 laborers died from malaria, yellow fever and landslides. The work was abandoned and resumed about a decade later by an American firm. Locks were incorporated to address the terrain. This was one of the largest and most difficult projects of all time, but the canal had an enormous impact on maritime shipping between the two oceans. But I digress.

The days spent aboard the ship were lazy and fun. I made friends with some of the crew and played checkers, chess or dominoes with them in their quarters and listened to their records. That particular year I decided to read the Bible from cover to cover. I read three chapters every day and five on Saturday. This pace allowed me to read the complete King James Version of the bible in a year. The most boring sections were the parts describing who begat whom ad infinitum. I have to admit I waded through a lot of difficult to understand sections but I did read EVERY word. It was not fun but it was definitely an accomplishment.

Once we crossed from the Mediterranean to the Atlantic, we hit an October storm. The ship was not fully loaded so it floated high on the surface of the water. It was tossed and rocked violently by each wave and we got so seasick that we thought being thrown overboard and drowning would have been a relief. The feeling resolved itself the next day when the storm abated and we were lucky to have calm seas for the rest of the journey.

The endless water as far as the eye could see began to get monotonous, so you can imagine our anticipation as we approached our new country. We were excited to wake up on that morning and see our first seagulls, a sign that we were finally approaching land. I felt like Christopher Columbus. Within a few hours we glimpsed land and a few hours later we passed Ellis Island (we did not stop), the Statue of Liberty and finally entered the East River. We docked in NYC on Columbus Day, 1958.

The next few hours were a blur as we passed through customs, filled out the necessary papers and received our coveted green card. Although the process was quick and efficient there was a minor issue, which affected me particularly. The naming system in Egypt is somewhat different than it is in America. Each child born in Egypt is given a first name only. Their second name would be his/her father's first name; the third name would be the grandfather's first name and so on. My father liked the sound of the name Mina, his grandfather's first name, so he gave me the middle name 'Mina'. Most Egyptians used three names: their given first name, their father's first name as their 'middle name' and their grandfather's first name as their 'last' name. This meant that our family's names were different from each other. To simplify this issue, we decided to use Mina as our family name. Because my given name was Rami Mina, I became Rami Mina Mina or Rami Mina Squared!! My new American friends teased me mercilessly. A few years later, I dropped one of the Mina's from my name as part of the citizenship process. My Egyptian full name was Rami Mina Ramses Riskalla Mina Latrouche Fakrak-Allah Carcour Abu-Hashish El-Assiuty. It seems easier to trace family histories with overlapping names than it is with the American family name system.

Once through customs, we caught a short cab ride to the YMCA in Manhattan. I marveled at the buildings and ubiquitous yellow cabs but I was totally disappointed with the new cars. They were not clean and shiny, as I had anticipated. It was Columbus Day, October 10th and it had just rained so New York was dark, cold and dirty - a bummer.

After we got settled at the "Y", we went out to explore NYC. Our cousins who had been there suggested we not miss seeing the Rockettes at Radio City Music Hall. We were lucky because it was not too far from the "Y". We soon found it and stood in a long line, which snaked all around the building. As we got closer to the entrance, I suspected it was a movie house and being super religious at the time, I told my parents I thought it was a sinful movie house and refused to go. They honored my wishes and we got a bite to eat instead and headed back to the "Y".

The next morning we headed to Chicago. My cousin Tawfik picked us up in New York City and drove us to our final destination. That first weekend, we stayed at a pension in La Grange, one of Chicago's suburbs. A pension is a large boarding house in which one rents rooms from the owner. The other residents were a father and two sons, who were approximately my age, and the lady who owned the house.

I mentioned to the guys that I had never seen a television in my life, so they decided to treat us with a typical American evening of eating pizza and watching TV. It sounded exciting because I didn't know what pizza was and I was going to see moving images at home on a real television. I didn't even care what we were going to see.

Evening came and we started watching a western on TV (I think it was "Have Gun Will Travel"). The anticipated pizza finally arrived. They opened the box and I discovered that pizza was nothing but bread topped with tomato sauce and cheese. I couldn't believe they made such a big fuss on something so ordinary. Of course pizza quickly became one of my favorite new American meals.

A few days later we rented a house on Ogden Avenue in La Grange. The house was close to the Burlington train station, which made it easy for my father to walk there and ride the train to work. La

Grange was a postcard American suburb with wide maple tree lined streets, big white houses and a small downtown shopping area. At that time of the year, the trees had turned bright red and orange colors. There were mounds of leaves along the sidewalks where the children played. Some mounds were burned and the smell of fall was in the air. It was gorgeous and met all my expectations.

We rented an unfurnished house, which had been vacant for a few months so the lawn was like an alfalfa field with knee high grass. My parent's first purchase was a lawn mower and seven beds, one for each of us. As I was mowing the lawn, I noticed a few injured baby rabbits scurrying away. A mother rabbit had nested in the tall grass and the mower inadvertently cut off the top and ears of a couple of them. We found the rest and moved them to a safer area.

I went to sleep in my new bed that first night exhausted and excited to be in America and woke up the next morning to find white salt like "stuff" covering the tree outside my window. At first, I thought it was a phenomenon peculiar to that tree but soon discovered that it was actually snow. I was a little disappointed because this snow was just a dusting of cold white powder instead of the beautiful symmetrical flakes I had envisioned.

My parents soon purchased the rest of the furniture and other necessities and began their new life in Chicago, while I went away to Broadview Academy about 50 miles away. School had just started and I entered school after Columbus Day weekend.

My new school looked bleak and ominous. The campus was composed of three buildings on top of a small hill in the middle of nowhere. One building housed the administration offices and classrooms, another was the boy's dormitory and the third housed the girl's dormitory, cafeteria and kitchen.

I was assigned to room with Jim Purple, a fellow senior. He helped me assimilate into my new environment by introducing me to several classmates, familiarizing me with school routines and showing me the campus. Everyone had to work a few hours a week to defray some of our expenses, as well as teach us good work ethics. My first job was washing breakfast pots and pans. I did not like work but the effort went a long way in teaching me humility.

It was a year of many firsts, some good, and some not so good. Living away from home was great. I liked my family, but I preferred my independence. Walking from our dorm to the cafeteria, then to classes in the blustery Illinois winter on an open hilltop, without proper attire was not so great. I didn't like walking in the snow without boots. I once mentioned that I needed some rubbers and everyone snickered. I didn't understand why they laughed at me but was too proud to ask. Much later I realized that rubbers had two meanings and I was not pleased that they took advantage of my ignorance.

On the other hand, my class work was very easy. The British system I came from was more rigorous so I sailed through my senior year with top grades and very little effort.   One of the month's highlight activities was "Town Nights". We went to the small neighboring town of La Fox for an evening of shopping and eating.   We gorged on 10-cent McDonald's hamburgers, french fries and shakes. At that time, the Big McDonald sign advertised, "More than 5 Million Sold".

The summer after high school, I worked as an orderly at Hinsdale Hospital and started dating Judith Davidson, who was incidentally voted the prettiest girl in our senior class. She too worked at Hinsdale and we used to make out in her car many nights after work. Our wild making-out sessions were limited to kissing and light petting because I was too afraid to go any further.

I used to take the midnight train home from Hinsdale to La Grange. One night I was a few minutes late, ran to the train station and found an empty station with no train or waiting people. I thought I missed the last one for the night. I called home to see if my father could pick me up. Unfortunately he was already in bed and was not too happy to be woken up. He said that he would pick me up in forty-five minutes. The train came a couple of minutes after I hung up. Now I was in a worse predicament. Should I wait for my father or hop the train and hope to make it home before he left? I chose the latter. I got off the train at La Grange and ran as fast as I could to our house. As I turned the corner onto our street, I saw my dad's car's taillights.... those ugly, 1959 Chevy eye-shaped taillights just pulling away from the stoplight. I paced our house waiting for a very angry father to return. He finally came in over an hour later and did not say a word. He grimly went to his room, put on his pajamas and returned to bed. I never heard another word about the incident. In hindsight, that silent treatment was more effective in making me feel guilty than anything else he could have said or done.

It is quite unfortunate that immigrating to the United States and all the associated changes came at the critical time for choosing a college and a lifetime career. I came from a system where the career choices were predetermined by your grades to one that was wide open in terms of colleges to attend and profession to choose. This was further complicated by the SDA religion. My parents were not knowledgeable enough to offer much advice, so I floundered my way through the maze of college applications and career choices.

At one point, I told my devout mother that I was interested in becoming a church minister. She encouraged me but my dad suggested I become an engineer like him. I registered at the University of Illinois on Chicago's Navy Pier and took general study classes. At the end of the first semester, my father changed jobs and the family moved to Rochester, NY. I moved with them and took some night classes at the University of Rochester to complete my first year of college.

The remainder of my college career was spent in two SDA colleges. Atlantic Union College (AUC) was located in South Lancaster, Massachusetts, about 60 miles west of Boston and Columbia Union College (CUC) was located in Takoma Park, Maryland. I graduated from CUC in May 1965 with a Biology major and a Chemistry minor.

Like college students everywhere, my college years were exciting, hard work and fun but not necessarily unique. I'm sharing the following experiences with you not to brag about my education or background, but to define the significant factors that shaped my life for years to come.

AUC and CUC were private colleges, fully accredited, with a student population of 800-1200 students. Most of us were SDAs and lived on campus. At that time, I was a devout SDA Christian and immersed myself in all church and school activities. Fortunately many of the incoming students attended Broadview Academy, so there were many old friends and familiar faces.

My college dorm at AUC was a neat state-of-the-art facility. Every four students occupied two rooms separated by a shared bathroom. We lived in the last room on the second floor. The guy in our adjacent room lived alone and his room was impeccable, always clean with plants and fresh flowers. I commented to my sloppy roommate that we should keep our room as clean as his. He informed me that impeccably clean rooms with plants implied the occupant was gay. I did not understand the concept and he explained in graphic detail. At first, I thought he was "leading me on" until I confirmed the phenomena independently. It's amazing that I didn't know anything about homosexuality until I was nineteen years old.

My college years were a blur of classes, interspersed with work, pranks and socializing. One of the required general courses was speech or oral reading. I chose oral reading expecting it to be less work than speech. Our teacher was a bland, nice older lady. I decided to try an experiment. Being a foreigner and relatively new to the United States I pretended to be weak in English and read that first segment with broken English and lots of hesitation. As the semester proceeded I became more fluent and read more naturally. It was a very difficult feat to propagate, but it worked. By the end of the semester I aced the class because I was the most improved. Both the teacher and I were happy with the results, but I still feel a little guilty.

I generally worked between twenty and forty hours per week, primarily to pay for my share of tuition and my car and gas. I worked a variety of jobs like mopping floors, washing dishes, working piece meal in a plastics stamping company as well as at a furniture building company, Harris Pine Mills, now defunct. On one occasion, I saw a Hyster fork lift unattended. Brash Rami hopped on without any training and knocked over a high stack of drawer bottoms. I was fired immediately. My most lucrative college job was waiting tables for high-end functions and banquets at the Washington DC hotels. The hotels hired local college students because it was cheaper than hiring union waiters. We were delighted to make $4.50 per hour and get all the free food we could eat.

I was interested in pursuing a career in medicine and as a result worked at Highland Hospital in Rochester, NY during the summers. I worked as a floor orderly, central supply technician, emergency room technician, as well as laboratory technician. There, I drew and analyzed blood samples. One of my worst experiences there happened while analyzing a few urine samples. I was also drinking a can of soda. Inadvertently I took a large gulp of a patient's urine sample instead of my soda. Let me inform you that urine is extremely salty!! I was repelled by my mistake and never ate or drank anything at the laboratory again.

I had two other unique jobs in college worth mentioning. The first was working the night shift at a mental ward of the local hospital. It was a college student's dream job. I could study all night, make hourly checks on the patients and report any anomalies to the head nurse. All went well until one night I walked into a patient's room. She was lying on the bed stark naked and had smeared poop all over everything. Naturally the nurse told me to clean it up and I immediately gagged, vomited and told her I could not do it. I was fired on the spot. I believe that episode led to my lifetime aversion to feces and was the reason I succeeded in going through life without changing any diapers.

The other job was working as an autopsy room technician, where I assisted the pathologist in weighing organs, washing out intestines (the smell was horrific) and finally depositing all the viscera in the body cavity and suturing it back together. It was a most interesting but macabre job.

I would be remiss not to include the major world event that occurred during my years at CUC: the assassination of President John F. Kennedy. It was a balmy November afternoon and I was playing tennis when one of the girls shouted out of her window that the president was shot. His death that evening cast a somber shadow over our campus and the world. Some of us attended the funeral procession on Pennsylvania Avenue. The crowd was enormous and packed so tightly, the only thing separating us was our clothes. In spite of all the people, it was an orderly and moving experience and one that remains seared in my memory.

The summer between my junior and senior year at CUC, all biology majors were required to take a six-week course at the college field station located in the Shenandoah Mountains of Virginia. It was a great experience taking field trips, watching birds in the woods, crossing streams, climbing mountains and being totally immersed in nature. Evenings were spent around campfires, telling stories and roasting marshmallows. One evening my best "friend", Ian Trace suggested we go snipe hunting. I didn't know what a snipe hunt was. One person sits under a tree at night holding a pillowslip and a flashlight. The others would quietly go into the woods and flush out the snipe (small birds) toward the flashlight, which are then trapped into the pillowslip. Being head strong, or foolhardy, I volunteered and was immediately chosen to hold the pillowslip. I sat there in the dark for a long time, before I finally gave up and sheepishly returned to camp. All my friends were warm happy, and laughing at my gullibility. I was a little embarrassed but that may have contributed to the development of a "thick skin" and a teasing personality.

On a more serious note, two factors happened during my senior year that were pivotal in shaking my faith in the SDA religion. The first was attending a class titled "Creation Vs. Evolution". I decided to take the course to cement my belief in the creationist ideologies. At the beginning of the semester, open-minded Prof. Lester Harris, indicated he was going to present the arguments objectively and each of us were to decide for ourselves which side made more sense. I was surprised to discover that it took "faith" to believe in either theory because both leave many unanswered questions. There are more facts on the side of evolution, so evolution is supported by more facts and creation requires more faith. More importantly, the theory of creation is <u>inconsistent</u> with well-established scientific observations. This was a huge revelation for me and caused me to doubt ALL the religious ideas that I have been exposed to for the previous fifteen years.

Another unrelated factor also came about during my senior year. A couple of my close friends asked if I would go to see the movie "Goldfinger" with them.

I was shocked that they would consider such a daring and sinful escapade. They indicated they had been to several movies and it was a great experience, and didn't cause anyone any harm. The church had taught us that we are "in this world, but not of this world", and for that reason we were not to go to movies and mingle with sinners. After some thorough soul searching, I decided to go and see for myself. Up to that point, I had demonized moviegoers in my mind, and was somewhat afraid of being with them. I found out that moviegoers were just normal people. I thoroughly enjoyed the film and did not notice any difference between moviegoers and the true Christians. Naturally this was the first of many trips to the theater. It's also ironic that I would end up with a career in the movie industry.

As I transitioned into the outside world and increased my exposure to work colleagues, neighbors and non-SDA individuals, I discovered that most were good people and not the scary "bad" people I had envisioned. On the contrary, they were more open minded, non-judgmental and generally much more well rounded than many of the SDAs I had known. It was not long after graduation that I totally renounced the faith and began to follow a more "normal" path.

Finding My Niche

I returned to Rochester after graduating from CUC in the spring of 1965 for two compelling reasons. The main one was my girlfriend Sue Ideman. I met her two years earlier, when we both worked at Highland Hospital. Although she was not a Seventh Day Adventist and was five years younger than me, I was madly infatuated with her. Also, since I was not accepted into medical school, I planned to work at one of the Rochester hospitals as I had done during the summers. I would take some courses at the University of Rochester then apply to medical school again the following year.

Within three months after returning to Rochester, Sue and I decided to elope because she was not quite 18 years old. We thought we would keep it a secret but once we got married, we told our parents immediately. I don't recall my parents' reaction but I do recall that her parents were shocked but took it calmly. They were more disappointed that they were not going to have a big wedding for their daughter and Mr. Ideman wouldn't have a chance to "walk her down the aisle".

We moved into a small apartment on Thurston Avenue and Sue got a job with my sisters, Samia and Mona in a mobile home toilet manufacturing company. At the same time I started working at the University of Rochester (U of R), as a research assistant to an eminent geneticist, Dr. Kaspari.

Dr. Kaspari went on a Sabbatical a few months after I joined his group, so I had a chance to work independently on extracting DNA from fruit flies (Drosophila Melanogaster). We were trying to cross breed them and affect a change in their eye color gene. This was in early 1966, before DNA extraction and analysis became commonplace. The assignment was interesting and more importantly, it allowed me to take free courses at the U of R.

The first few months were exciting and fun but before I knew it, reality set in and Sue became pregnant.

Naturally, family and friends were excited with the news and we started planning for the new arrival. A baby shower was planned for a Sunday afternoon in February of 1966 at Sue's parents house. It had started snowing that morning, so instead of dropping Sue off, I decided to wait at their house to take her home after the shower.

The snow continued through the afternoon and by the time everyone was ready to leave, the snowstorm had turned into a severe blizzard with white out conditions. Everyone decided to wait out the storm before driving home.

Unfortunately, radio stations began broadcasting road and school closings. Street after street became impassable and closed to traffic. Before long, the whole city had shut down except for critical services.

There we were, my new father-in-law and myself, with several great looking, gussied up, well dressed young ladies, "stuck" together in a house.

At first, it was sort of fun. We played scrabble and monopoly, had more snacks and everyone was polite and friendly. It soon became apparent that no one was going to be able to leave until the next day. Some became anxious but most took it in stride.

We woke up the next day to find out that the blizzard had not subsided. We could not open the front door because the snow was higher than the door. The possibility of going home that day became remote at best. Everyone became irritable and the initial politeness vanished. The situation was exacerbated by the depletion of our food, drinks and cigarettes. Almost everyone smoked and the dwindling supply of cigarettes was associated with a proportional increase in panic, anger and profanity.

On the third day, the sun came out and my father-in-law and I dug a path from their front door to the street. We wore makeshift snowshoes made out of paint trays strapped to our shoes and walked on top of the snow to the neighborhood grocery store. We bought cigarettes, bread and milk and returned to a cheering crowd. I was surprised that a bunch of great looking and polite young ladies could turn into untamed, foul-mouthed shrews in just a few days.

The storm of "Sixty Six" was one of the most severe in Rochester's history. All schools and businesses were shut down for three days. Many policemen, firemen and hospital employees got stuck working around the clock for several days.

Dianne was born exactly nine months from the time we got married. I took Sue to Highland Hospital early the morning of March 26, 1966, full of anticipation of meeting our new child. It was a particularly difficult delivery and I recall many women screaming with pain and angry with their husbands "for doing this to them". I was thankful Sue was not one of them. I left for a few minutes to take a break and returned shortly afterwards to find that Sue had delivered our beautiful first child, Dianne Marie. I had hoped for a girl and my wishes were granted.

Sue did not work the first few months after Dianne was born and I needed a higher paying job to support my new family. I applied to work as a research assistant at Kodak and was hired to work in the analytical sciences division for the grand sum of $77.00 per week. I supplemented our income by working as a medical technologist at the Highland Hospital Chemistry Laboratory in the evenings.

We also needed a two-bedroom apartment. Fortunately brand new "low income" apartments just became available. We applied, got accepted and moved into our brand new two-bedroom apartment the same day and time as the Buerkles (who would become close family friends) moved into theirs. I remember Joanie holding Julie and Sue holding Dianne while we both signed our leases.

Most of the tenants were young professionals, just entering the workforce and had little babies, just like us. I played poker with the guys every Friday night. We all played charades went out to dinner several times a month and formed many lifetime relationships.

Unfortunately, some of us began to experience some marital stress. I detected that Sue was not very happy and was not sure if it was because I had two jobs and was gone much of the time or if she was influenced by her mother, who did not like me very much. The situation began to deteriorate and eventually we decided to try a two-week separation. Sue went to her mother's house with Dianne and I stayed at the apartment.

Before long we reconciled our differences and got back together. Meanwhile, I had decided to pursue a PhD degree in Chemistry, after which I would return to Kodak. Sue agreed to join me in a new life away from Rochester. I chose the University of Arizona in Tucson because the weather was superior to Rochester's and we would be 2500 miles away from my mother-in-law's influence.

We packed our belongings into a U-haul trailer, said our good-byes to our friends and neighbors and began our cross-country trip to Tucson. We arrived in time for the new school year and rented an apartment in the U of A student-housing complex at the base of Mount Lemon.

I began my studies, started a part time job at the university and supplemented it by another job delivering newspapers to carriers from midnight to four AM. Sue also got a job at TMC hospital as a medical technician. By necessity we hardly saw each other because someone had to take care of Dianne while the other was working.

This put undue strain on a fragile marriage and before long Sue wanted another separation. I was somewhat surprised because I thought we were on the road to recovery. I don't recall anything happening that would precipitate the desire to split up.

Moreover, stress began to take its toll on my studies and I found myself struggling to maintain passing grades. Sue eventually informed me that she wanted a divorce and said that if I didn't leave, she would. I decided to move because I didn't want her and Dianne to be out looking for another place to live.

One night I told Sue that I wanted to see Dianne and to my surprise, she refused so I went to visit anyway, but no one was home. I opened the refrigerator and found a few bottles of beer, two dirty dishes in the sink and other evidence that someone else, in addition to Sue and Dianne, was using my apartment.

The signs may have been there all along, but it was a surprise and shock to me. I became very despondent. I didn't think the future held any promise and I wanted to end it all. I found some lighter fluid under the sink, which I proceeded to drink. I don't know how long I was out but I woke up in a hospital just having had my stomach pumped out. My mother flew to Tucson the next day. A few days later, my mother and I headed back to Rochester and I didn't know what the future held.

Needless to say this was the absolute low point of my life. I had returned home a complete loser: I left my career type job, flunked out of school and lost my wife and daughter. My self worth was totally shot. The first order of business was to get a psychiatric evaluation. I expected months of treatments. I had a one-hour consultation and the doctor told me that my reaction was perfectly normal considering the circumstances. He said I did not need treatment and to go and put my life back together.

Upon returning to Rochester, I went back to Kodak. Fortunately, my work record was good and I was reinstated without losing any seniority. I spent the next few months totally immersed in my work and happy to begin rebuilding my life.

On the marriage front, I found that Sue had also moved back to Rochester and was living with her parents. I tried to call her many times but she would not talk to me. Her parents finally told me that if I wanted to contact her, I would have to do so through her attorney.

Within a few weeks I was served with divorce papers on the basis of "irreconcilable differences". The next few months were frustrating at best, because all negotiations were done through lawyers whose interest was to prolong the case with the meter running.

Sue knew my close relationship with Dianne and used that to inflict emotional duress in an attempt to get back at me. I did not understand or know what happened that precipitated such strong anger!! She succeeded in convincing the court that I was a potential threat to Dianne and my visitation rights were limited to two hours a week at her parent's house under supervision. The visitations were stressful at best and did nothing to foster any kind of meaningful father-daughter relationship.

Sue retained Rochester's most aggressive and experienced attorney while mine was mediocre at best. Despite all efforts by my attorney and character references by colleagues and supervisors from Kodak, the court issued the divorce and all judgments ended up in her favor. I believe that many divorces granted in NY in the late sixties were biased towards the mother and my case was no exception. My visitation rights continued to be two hours per week at her parent's house and a reasonable alimony was awarded. To add insult to injury, the court decided that I was to pay all court fees including Sue's attorney's fees, which turned out to be double my own attorney's fees.

Just one month after our divorce decree, Sue moved back to Tucson and took Dianne with her. This was a devastating blow for me because Dianne and I had been very close. Her move out of state left a tremendous emptiness in my heart. Any attempts to get the visitation rights changed were met with resistance. In fact, I adopted Julie Buerkle as my "surrogate daughter" and we remained close for a long time. I discovered that the Pima County, Arizona courts would decide the visitation rights issue. At that time I was financially and emotionally drained and decided to let the matter rest and take it up once I got on my feet. A few months later Sue married the guy who, I think, precipitated the divorce.

Once our divorce decree was finalized, I focused my attention on rebuilding my life. My primary objectives were to establish my credibility at work and to rebuild my social network in Rochester.

I spent a lot of time with my sisters and their husbands and dated many women, some for their looks, others for their cooking ability and some for other reasons!! I learned how to play bridge and played golf and tennis several times a week.

I also met another Egyptian, Tony Ateya. Tony was my age; also single and worked down the hall from my lab at Kodak. Tony and I soon became good friends and shared many evenings drinking, talking and picking up girls.

My life was on the mend and my financial situation was improving so I took this opportunity to pursue one of my lifelong desires, to learn how to fly airplanes. I joined the Rochester Flying Club, which had about one hundred members and owned six airplanes. These were available to club members on a first come basis. Fortunately, not all members were frequent fliers or active pilots so plane availability was not a problem. We reserved planes on a first come basis, paid a nominal hourly rate for gas, maintenance and insurance and took off.

That was the easy part. Obtaining a private pilot's license on the other hand, was a very involved, expensive and difficult process. The three primary requirements were to obtain an FAA medical certificate, pass a written test and finally pass a flight test given by an FAA approved examiner.

The medical certificate certified that one had the physical ability and mental stability to control and fly an airplane.

The written test was more difficult and required months of study. One had to demonstrate proficiency in aeronautics, FAA regulations, the use of flight charts for VFR (visual flight rules) navigation, radio communication procedures, use of weather reports and forecasts, weight and balance computations and a thorough knowledge of aerodynamics, power-plants and aircraft systems.

The actual flight instruction in an airplane was the most fun, expensive and comprehensive. The requirements included at least forty hours of flight time, twenty of which must be under the direction of an authorized instructor and a minimum ten hours of solo flight.

The specific requirements included night flying, cross-country flights of over 150 nautical miles, several hours of flying instruments, without outside visibility and many others.

Needless to say, all the effort that went into obtaining that license opened the door to unparalleled excitement and fun. The feeling I got as I obtained the clearance for takeoff pushed in the throttle and went faster and faster until I became airborne was truly exhilarating. For me, this great feeling was analogous to making a perfect golf shot, hooking and reeling in a large tuna and of course reaching a climax when I was twenty.

Most pilot's favorite pastime is to sit around the clubhouse and recount their flying experiences and I would be delinquent if I don't mention at least one of my more harrowing flights.

It was an early spring weekend. Barbara (the girl I married a few years later), my sister Samia and her husband Dan and I decided to fly from Rochester to Washington DC in the Rochester Flying Club's newest airplane, a brand new American Yankee Traveler.

The weather forecast was perfect, I plotted and filed a flight plan and made the appropriate weight calculation and we were well within the acceptable envelope. I completed the visual inspection of all flight surfaces and we were off without a hitch. The sun was out and the visibility was great. We made it to our destination airport in one of DC's suburbs on time and without any problems. It was a great flight.

American Yankee Traveler

After landing, a small crowd gathered around the airplane, because that model was brand new and this particular airplane was one of the first ones off the assembly line.

We tied the airplane down and left for town, where we stayed with a friend. We returned to the airport on an equally bright Monday morning to ideal flight conditions.

After gassing up, filing the appropriate flight plan and completing all the necessary pre-flight procedures, we started our journey back. As we lifted off the runway, I noticed a hedge of trees in front of us, which we had to clear. We had plenty of airspeed to clear the trees but as we approached, the stall-warning buzzer began to beep. Samia and Dan asked what that was and I calmly told them the buzzer was a normal climb indicator while I was sweating on the inside. Barbara knew what the sound indicated and she too was worried, but sat there stoically keeping her fear under control. The only way to avert a stall was to increase speed. As we approached the trees, it became very dicey. The stall buzzer became louder, the throttle was full open and I could not increase power to climb over the trees. The only way to avert a stall was to put the nose down towards the trees to increase airspeed. I decided to use a slingshot approach, not knowing whether I had the distance to do it or whether it was feasible at all. It was my only option. I put the nose down and increased airspeed just enough to quiet the buzzer. At the very last moment, I pulled up the yoke and we managed to skim the treetops and finally climb. That was one of the most frightful experiences in my career as a pilot.

A few months later, a fellow club member experienced the same problem and actually crashed the plane. Fortunately there were no injuries. It was determined that an airplane design flaw caused the problem and that particular model was taken out of production.

Love and Marriage – Reboot

I met Barbara, the girl I would marry, in a circuitous and unexpected way. One Friday night, Tony Ateya went to the Shakespeare Room, the Rochester hangout for those of us looking to hook up. He met a pretty girl named Sue Kromback. Apparently they hit it off because the next day he told me he met the girl he was going to marry. Sure enough he and Sue started to go out regularly and sometimes double dated with whomever I happened to be dating and me.

Sue lived with one of her college friends, Barbara, in an apartment on Goodman Street. They had an alcoholic neighbor who frequently asked them to buy alcohol for him and often became unmanageable if they refused. One fateful night, Tony, Sue, my date and I were going out for the evening. Fortunately for me, Barb tagged along because she didn't want to stay alone at home with the unpredictable neighbor.

We went to a bowling alley and I sent my date to get a bowling ball. While she was gone, I asked Barbara about her plans for the next day. She said she was going to wash her car. I said I was doing the same and invited her to come to my parent's house so we can wash both of our cars in their driveway. She accepted. After bowling, we all went to dinner and finally to my date's house for a nightcap.

The evening went by quickly. I'm afraid I paid more attention to Barbara than to my friend. Barbara and I got some of the awkward "get to know you" conversation out of the way in a relaxed non-committal environment.

The next day Barbara came to our house, we washed the cars and had dinner with my family. My parents met Barbara in a pleasant informal setting before we ever thought of getting serious. Initially, neither of us thought this relationship was going anywhere. I thought Barbara was too aloof and she thought I was too silly (the first time I met her I jumped in a puddle to splash her). More importantly though, a few minutes after we met I asked her in French if she would go to bed with me. She did not say no, so I knew we had "chemistry".

Barbara and I spent a lot of time together in those early days. I was impressed by her quiet but strong personality. She was intelligent and did not feel the need to prove it. She was gorgeous, yet grounded, and I rarely (no, never) heard her say anything negative about anybody. The more I knew her, the more I realized how great she was. Very early in our relationship I knew beyond any doubt that I wanted to spend the rest of my life with her. One weekend, while camping in Toronto with a couple of my Kodak colleagues, she and I were lying in a tent in our separate sleeping bags. She stirred and I whispered to see if she was awake. She was. I asked her if she would marry me and to my delight, she said yes.

We embarked on all the normal wedding preparation details. We knew we wanted a church wedding but which church? Barbara was a Catholic and I was a Protestant who was previously married. Unfortunately, we asked for advice from a very conservative priest who informed us that since my previous marriage was to a Catholic, it could not be annulled and we could not be married in the Catholic Church. I was somewhat relieved because I really did not believe in the Catholic faith. Barbara too was beginning to question her Catholic upbringing and all its traditional dogma.

We considered other Christian denominations that we could both accept and settled on the Episcopalian faith. It was close enough to Catholicism to make it comfortable for Barbara and liberal enough to make it palatable for me. We met a young pastor who guided us through a series of classes on marriage then he agreed to marry us.

A few months before our wedding, my mother began to feel ill. We initially thought she had the flu but when the symptoms continued, her doctor suggested we take her to the hospital for further testing. She entered the hospital in April. Within a couple of weeks the doctors suspected she had cervical cancer and decided to operate. Unfortunately the cancer was fast spreading and had metastasized through several vital organs. She passed away prematurely a month before our wedding at the age of 56. This was devastating to all of us because she was a wonderful mother. Later on we discovered that every one of her five children thought that he or she was our mother's favorite. I don't know how she accomplished that. We discussed postponing the wedding with her and she insisted we go through with the plans. It was sad because she had already purchased her wedding dress and was not going to get the chance to wear it. On the other hand, I was thankful that Barbara had a chance to know that great lady.

Our somber wedding took place at the University of Rochester Interfaith Chapel on a bright sunny July day. We wrote and said our own vows to each other. My vow was: "Barbara, with this ring I pledge my everlasting love to you, in good times and in bad. I will care for you and grow with you and share my life with you, respecting your individuality as you respect mine. As you wear this ring, remember that my love goes with you always." And Barbara's vow was: "Rami, with this ring I marry you because I love you and want to spend my life with you. I'll always be at your side, physically and spiritually, sharing your joys and sorrows, respecting you and growing with you. This ring is a symbol of my love, which will always be with you." Our vision was to retain our individualities while going through life as a tight unit. As I look back on our many years as a couple, I feel that we accomplished our goal.

A reception followed at the Logan Party House in Rochester with about one hundred of our closest friends and relatives. We did not hire a band and refrained from dancing. Also, several of my relatives witnessed our marriage but skipped the reception in honor of my mother's recent passing. It was a very nice but restrained celebration. Following the reception, we left for our honeymoon in Quebec City.

The first few years of marriage were full of blissful activity. We set up house in a two-bedroom apartment in the desirable Park Avenue section of Rochester. That area attracted young professionals because it was centrally located and had many old mansions, which were converted to apartments. It was also within walking distances to the Planetarium, Art Gallery, Museum of Natural History and many trendy cafes and restaurants.

Beside Tony and Sue Ateya, we reconnected with one of Barbara's college acquaintances, Marilyn and her husband Jean Guy Roy. She had just returned from a Peace Corp assignment in Africa. Other friends included Joan and Dan Buerkle, who were my old neighbors in my previous marriage. I mention these people because they have all remained close friends throughout our lives.

These early marriage years were exciting for all of us. Our work lives were challenging, new and exciting. We were fresh out of school and were ready to change the world. I will describe my career in the corporate world in a separate chapter.

None of us had any children living with us except for the Buerkles, so essentially every weekend was filled with parties, playing cards and word games, as well as plenty of golf and tennis. We often went on weekend camping trips to one of the many state parks in the area.

Allegheny State Park Camping Gang

Susan, Mary and Me

Not all was work and fun however, because many of us also attended graduate school. Barbara attended the University of Rochester to pursue her master's degree in Elementary Education and I attended the Rochester Institute of Technology culminating in a master's degree in Chemistry.

There were many nights when Barb and I stayed up studying or writing, dead tired after a full day of work and school, only to wake up the next day and do it all over again. We frequently envied my sisters and their husbands, who went to work, had a good night's rest and woke up refreshed without the stress of classes, exams and papers. In retrospect, all that hard work while we were young with the stamina to do it paid huge dividends in later life.

Early in our marriage, Barb and I decided to put off having children until we finished graduate school, had a few years to get to know each other and, more importantly, became financially and emotionally ready to start a family.

By the time we completed graduate school, Marilyn and Guy had just put in an offer on their first house, after searching for more than a year.

We also anticipated buying a house the following year when we would have saved enough money for the down payment. We started looking, expecting it would take us that long to find one. Fortunately or unfortunately, we found a house we liked almost immediately. It was a three bedroom, fifteen hundred square foot center entrance colonial in Perinton NY, one of the suburbs southeast of Rochester.

We put in an offer for $35,000, never expecting it to be accepted. To our surprise it was. Now we were faced with the task of finding a six thousand dollar down payment. We borrowed the bulk of it from my father and Barbara's uncle and repaid the loans that first year. We were at the right time in the right place because the value of our new house increased by $8000 that first year, more than the amount we would have saved had we waited.

Our first house

Eager to play the role of lawn-mowing suburbanites, we fell right into the norm of buying a small Pinto station wagon and acquiring a puppy, a salt and pepper miniature schnauzer we named Gimli after a dwarf in J.R.R. Tolkien's, <u>The Hobbit</u>. For the first few days after we brought Gimli home, she never barked and we began to suspect we had a "defective" dog. That was wishful thinking because within a few weeks she was more comfortable in her new environment, started yapping and never stopped.

As far as Dianne was concerned, that emptiness I felt on her departure from Rochester never went away. As the weeks dragged into months and the months into years, it got harder and harder to reconnect with her because my emotions were still raw and I did not want to face the anticipated court battles, fearing they would re-open the wounds. Dianne had entered kindergarten but was registered in her stepfather's last name. This was both illegal and frustrating because I did not have any way to challenge the decision. That name remained with her until she got married and changed it to her current name. I had nothing to do with any decisions regarding her education and had very little if any influence on her life in spite of the tremendous desire to do so.

About that same time, I got a letter from Sue indicating that she and her husband intended to adopt Dianne. They initiated the court proceedings.

She indicated that if I accepted, all my responsibilities as well as child support payments would stop. I categorically refused and immediately retained a Tucson attorney who was successful in terminating the adoption proceedings and reinstating much more equitable visitation rights. The Tucson courts ordered that Dianne would come to Rochester and spend a month with us every summer.

This arrangement worked very well. Barbara, my new bride and I looked forward to her visits and I think Dianne enjoyed the change. As one would expect, the first few visits were a little tense because we had to establish our new relationships, but we adapted quickly and had a chance to settle in before our other children were born. Dianne was the big sister and was there to welcome them into our family. Dianne joined us every summer from the time she was seven years old until she was about sixteen, when she began working summers and was too busy with the typical teenage activities to continue our summer visits.

Now that Dianne had become an integral part of our family, we had our house, a dog and a station wagon, the only thing missing was a baby and we were ready. I was mowing the lawn one Saturday afternoon and Barbara was running errands. She came home, looked out of an upstairs window and announced that she had just returned from the doctor and found out that she was pregnant. JUBILATION!!! The exciting news initiated a tremendous amount of activity in our little household. We immediately spread the word and began preparations for the baby's arrival.

We knew the baby would arrive around Christmas and hoped it would come before the New Year for tax purposes. In those days, there was no ultrasound so we could not predetermine whether it was going to be a boy or girl. I was hoping it would be a girl to partially fill the void left by Dianne. Prior to that, we had always referred to our future children as Jennifer and Geoffrey but when reality set in, those names were abandoned. We liked names starting with J and wanted to make them unique, yet easy to say and recognize. One day while driving home, we were sounding out names like Jelima, Jenica, Jetira...etc. Jessica popped up and we both immediately liked it. We decided to give her an Egyptian middle name, Jihann, after president Sadat's wife's name. Jessica was not a popular name at the time or so we thought. We must have both subconsciously heard it before because once our Jessica arrived; it was not unique at all. It was that year's most popular girl's name. We chose Jessica Jihann.

Jessica arrived December 27, 1975. She was a full term, perfectly formed baby girl weighing 4 lbs. 15 oz. The obstetrician, Dr. Wax told us that now we have a cement wedge. We often thought of that because it was true figuratively and literally. Every time we hugged, there was little Jessica trying to "wedge" her way between us.

As soon as the baby was born the doctor handed her to me. Holding her that first time was a pleasant warm sensation and I thought she was THE most beautiful baby in the world. I really did not want to hand her over to her mother.

As Barbara and Jessica were wheeled out of the delivery room, Jessica was fully alert, looking all around, examining her new world and moving her little lips in a sucking like motion. She was surprisingly alert and relaxed considering the ordeal she had just experienced.

I left mother and baby to rest while I went shopping for the customary chocolates, cigars, and two roses, one red and one white for my girls. I was on cloud nine and could not wait to return to the hospital for another peek at our new baby.

The next day I went to work, spread the news and distributed the chocolates and cigars. One of my colleagues noted that the five pound box of chocolates weighed more than the baby!!

Barbara's mother came to Rochester to help take care of Jessica for a few days. That first week at home with the baby must have been quite stressful because one day I came home to find Barbara, her mother and Jessica crying their hearts out. I immediately took Jessica, gently rocked her and suggested that Barb and her mom should take long relaxing baths and leave

Jessica and me alone. Within half an hour, everyone was happy and calm.

Jessica partially filled the emptiness left when Dianne was taken to Tucson. As a result, from the time she was a tiny baby, I took her with me everywhere. I took her on Saturday morning errands, to visit friends and even quick hops to the store for milk or bread.

Jessica was quite fickle. Sometimes she felt close to me and did not want anything to do with her mother but within a few days, her allegiance would shift and the situation was reversed. She also developed an unusual attachment to rubber gloves, which she referred to as "ba". Rubber gloves became her security blanket. She went to sleep each night sucking her thumb and holding her "ba". It was actually more practical than a pacifier or blanket because any rubber glove would do. If we happened to leave hers at home, it was very easy to find another.

Jessica was precocious as a toddler. She had more than a two hundred-word vocabulary by the time she was eighteen months old and I wrote them all down. She also had a very active imagination. She talked about her imaginary friend named Tony. One day Jessica, Tony and I were riding in the car and I pretended to set Tony on my shoulder. The window was open and Tony fell out as we were going around a bend. Jessica got upset and insisted I stop the car and go back to find him. I finally stopped, picked him up and cleaned him off before she finally calmed down. Years later I asked her what Tony looked like and she described him in great detail as being about eight inches tall, with long white hair and blue overalls, similar to a garden gnome.

A couple of years after Jessica was born we wanted a larger house. We looked at a few developments and poured over hundreds of plans. We found a developer in Mendon, a suburb of Rochester, who was amenable to building a custom house on one of his lots if we were willing to work with his suppliers and subcontractors. We chose a one-acre lot backing up to woods in a very nice area of the Mendon Farms Development.

An architect designed a 2100 square foot center entrance colonial for us. The design was approved and building began on our new house in mid-1976. By that time Dianne had become an integral part of our growing family again. One afternoon, we loaded Jessica, Dianne and Gimli into our station wagon and went to inspect the building progress. The fireplace foundation between the living and family room was a huge pit extending from the first floor to the basement. Dianne was fooling around and dropped her flip-flops in the fireplace pit. Unfortunately it had no access. The only way to retrieve them was to fish them out using a fishing pole. I drove the ten miles to our old house, brought back a fishing rod and retrieved the flip-flops before dark.

We all piled in the car and drove home again. When we were almost home, we discovered that Gimli was not with us. By that time the sun had set, the stars emerged and it was completely dark. We wondered how we were going to find our dog. As we turned the corner into the darkened path, which was to become our new street, Gimli was sitting exactly where the car had been, waiting for us to return for her. She was a clever dog and was as happy to see us, as we were to see her.

Soon after we moved into our Mendon house, we started thinking about a little sibling for Jessica. We agonized over whether to wait a year or two to improve our financial state or to try again soon and have both kids closer together in age. We decided to stop contraceptives and let "nature" answer the question. "Fertile Myrtle" and "Herm the Sperm" immediately obliged and Matthew was born almost nine months to the day from the time we made that fruitful decision.

Most babies born to our respective families were girls so we were fully prepared to welcome another little girl into our family. You can imagine our surprise and delight when this scrawny little frog-like boy appeared. Matthew was a much calmer and quieter baby than Jessica. From the time he was born, he liked to cuddle and suck his thumb. Early on he developed a funny habit of rubbing our thumbnails while he sucked his thumb and sat on our laps. Matthew was a very good-looking baby and was a lot less verbal than his sister, typical of most boys with older sisters. He had difficulty verbalizing his thoughts. He did show incredible resourcefulness by his many attempts to get his thoughts across. At one point he was trying to describe a "railing". Difficult to say for anyone, let alone an eighteen month old. He tried to describe the railing at least four different ways before he finally walked to our stair railing and pointed to it.

On another occasion, we were all in the car and he saw a boom crane. I guess he and his little friends had discussed it. The problem was he called it "boon prain" and we didn't know what he was talking about. Again he tried several ways to describe it. He failed, got mad and said to forget it. On the way back, he saw it again and pointed to it and said that was the boon prain he saw. I said "Oh! You mean the boom crane!!" In utter frustration he insisted it was called a boon prain and that he was not going to talk to me again.

We consciously tried to treat both children the same way in terms of gender-neutral toys and activities. It was obvious that they acted in traditional ways in spite of all our efforts. Two incidents illustrate the point.

I usually performed minor car maintenance myself and the kids were always in the garage with me. When they were about two years old, I handed each of them a wrench and described what I was doing. Jess held the wrench and observed from a distance. Matt, on the other hand, got his wrench and weaseled his way between the car and me. He was totally involved.

The second incident occurred when Jessica was about five and Matt about two and a half. We had a wild outdoor cat that liked to sleep on top of the garage door when it was open! One Saturday afternoon we went shopping and closed the garage door not knowing the cat was there. We returned to find the cat's body sprawled and hanging from the top of the closed garage door with her head still inside. Jessica saw that gruesome sight, screamed and ran inside the house. When we opened the garage door, the dead cat fell to the ground and rigor mortis had set in. Its mouth was open and its front legs were stretched out in an unnatural angle. Matt watched quietly, seriously and intently. I told Matt that the cat died and I was going to bury it. We went to the back of our property for the burial but it was the middle of winter and the ground was frozen. Matt and I put the dead cat in the tractor cart and drove to one of the many empty fields around our house to dispose of it. Matt was totally quiet as he watched me toss it in a field some distance from our house. That was a mistake because on the ride home he wanted to know what was going to happen to the cat. I told him she died and was going to see God in heaven. He wondered whether heaven was in the field and asked many more questions such as: Why was its mouth open? Why were its legs stretched out? What is dead? Etc. The questions continued for a few weeks, to the point that Barbara and I became concerned and asked his pediatrician whether that was normal. He assured us it was. Jessica on the other hand screamed, cried, got it out of her system and never mentioned it again. Jessica lived up to expectations by being emotional and Matthew also lived up to expectations by being analytical. I'm sure I'm going to be challenged by many who don't agree with this characterization.

As the children matured, it became apparent that our efforts to minimize gender tendencies were unsuccessful. Jessica however, is very pragmatic and Matthew is sensitive and empathetic but that may be related to their personalities and not to gender differences.

When Jessica was just a few months old, one of Barbara's colleagues noted that she seemed extra alert and bright. She asked if she could test her IQ using Slosson Intelligence Test (SIT) for children and adults. It is not totally accurate at 3 months old but is a good indicator. Jess' IQ was fairly high and I decided to acquire the test so I could administer it as the baby grew. The tester observed and/or asked the subject many questions and the test ended when the subject missed ten questions in a row.

I tested both kids periodically and discovered that it was fairly accurate throughout. Jessica and Matthew had equally high scores but with a significant difference. Jessica answered most questions correctly to a certain point after which she missed ten in fairly quick succession. This indicated that she was a "traditional" thinker. Matthew's answers were more erratic. He missed several easy questions then answered the next one correctly. He would sometimes miss seven or eight questions in a row and then get the next one right. As a result, the test continued. This indicated that Matthew's knowledge and/or thought processes were less structured. This proved to be the case because Jessica excelled all the way through school and Matthew's brilliance blossomed well after his early twenties.

Early into our marriage, Barbara and I began a summer vacation tradition. We wanted our vacations to be both rejuvenating and sociable so we generally vacationed with one or more other families. The guys did "guy things", the girls did "girl things" and the children had playmates.

Several vacations were spent in Sebago Lake in Maine. My sister Samia and her family and our close friends, the DeMotts, accompanied us. We rented three adjacent cabins on a private beach on a quiet cove. One year we organized an Olympic week competition. We competed in volleyball, baseball, swimming races, holding our breath under water, jarts and a few other activities. Naturally these were all handicapped so everyone had an even chance to win. On another vacation we produced and acted in a Robinson Crusoe movie. It took the whole vacation to complete and provided many fond memories. The lobster dinners (two steamed lobsters, corn on the cob and Boston baked beans) available at lobster shacks for five dollars were luscious.

A few other vacations were spent in the Adirondacks Mountains and the Thousand Islands. My brother-in-law, Dan and I loved to fish. We woke up at dawn and fished for a few hours. The kids usually woke up while we were gone and my sister had to wake up early to take care of them. This made her furious with Dan because she liked to sleep late, especially on "her" vacation. They finally reached a compromise. We could fish every morning provided we returned before 9:00 am. We hardly ever made it back on time but always adjusted our watches appropriately and she never suspected.

Another vacation favorite was Nantucket Island off the coast of Massachusetts. There, we vacationed with the Ateyas and the Roys. We generally drove to Cape Cod and loaded our cars on the ferry for our two-hour trip across the sound. Nantucket was an old whaling village with many upscale mansions and surrounded by beautiful beaches. We spent many hours swimming, boating and playing word games. After two or three summers of renting different houses for a week or two, we decided to look into a timeshare. We found a great spot and paid $10,000 for the right to use a two-bedroom condo during the first and second week of every July. We could rent it or exchange it with other timeshares in the "Interval Ownership Club". We bought it to ensure a pleasant rental rather than as an investment. As luck would have it, we were transferred to California one year later. We were fortunate because another developer wanted to purchase the complex to build a bigger resort. Our fellow owners retained a lawyer to negotiate the sale and we ended up selling our share for $40,000, a four-fold increase in two years.

In 1983 we relocated from Rochester to Los Angeles. We maintained our relationship with Dianne by phone calls and visits whenever her schedule permitted. One summer she brought her high school boyfriend, Dale Tattersall, to meet us.

A couple of years later, Dale and Dianne decided to get married.   We were all happy for Dianne especially since she was marrying such an outstanding person.   During one fateful phone conversation I approached the touchy subject of who was going to "walk her down the aisle", her stepfather or myself. Our memories vary on exactly what was said but the end result was that I could not attend her wedding. I told her that when she had her own daughter, she would understand my feelings.   Unfortunately, we became totally estranged for a few more years.

Tara, Dianne's little girl was born a few years later.   Not surprisingly, I got a call from Dianne indicating that she considered families to be important and she wanted to re-establish a relationship with Barbara and me but not rehash and reopen old wounds.   We accepted them with open arms.

Within the first few years of their marriage, Dianne, Tara and Dale moved to Simi Valley, just a few miles away from us.   Soon afterwards, she presented us with two other gorgeous grand daughters, Alexa and Jenna. It's ironic that in spite of the rough patches, our relationship has grown stronger over the years. In fact Barbara and I are as close to Dianne's family as anyone and that was one of the primary reasons we decided to move to Temecula.

When we first moved to Los Angeles, I joined a group of people from the motion picture industry who chartered a deep-sea fishing boat one Saturday a month. Matthew joined me from the time he was about four years old. We boarded at dawn; fished all day in the Channel Islands, off the coast of Santa Barbara and returned home about six pm with enough fish to feed an army. The monthly fishing trips were upgraded first to three-day, then to five-day Deep Sea fishing vacations.

When Jessica was in her final year at the University of California in San Diego we often visited her on weekends. On one occasion I went to the wharf to watch the returning fishing boats with their tuna catches. I could not believe my eyes! There were hundreds of huge fish, all caught over the weekend by the exhausted but happy fishermen. I discovered a late cancellation on one of the charters and immediately booked a three-day trip for the following weekend. I spent the next week reading everything I could about deep sea fishing, acquiring the necessary gear and practicing casting in our back yard.

I arrived at the dock the following Saturday morning to find the gleaming EXCEL, a luxury 125-foot fishing yacht with sixteen staterooms, each with a sink and two bunk beds. The vessel is equipped with its own desalination plant; quick-freeze fish hold, seven showers and a large enough galley to seat all thirty-two passengers. Breakfast, lunch and dinner were comparable to those served on luxury cruises and snacks were always available. My favorite was fresh sushi made from just-caught blue fin or yellow fin tuna. We fished, ate and drank all day; played poker or watched movies at night then fell into bed for our much-needed rest. We woke up early the next morning to a deckhand shouting: "Hook up". He was telling the captain to slow down because we found a school of tuna and someone hooked a fish. We jumped out of bed, baited our rods and put them in the water before we were fully awake.

The Excel

Nothing is quite as rewarding as feeling the large tuna pick up the live anchovy or sardine on your hook. There is no doubt when that happens because it typically charges off at more than 30 mph, making the reel scream. You wait a few seconds, flip the drag, put your thumb firmly on the spool and set the hook. Now the real fun begins. You usually fish with 35 to

40 lb. test line and the fish could easily weigh twice that much, so setting the drag correctly is critical. Set it too tightly and the fish will snap your line; set it too loosely and it will "spool" you, take all your line, and also snap it. The idea is to set it tightly enough to tire the fish and allow you to reel it in as it rests. The fight is solely between you and the monster fish. You reel it in as it rests and you rest as it gets another burst of energy and takes your line. If the hook does not come off your line or the line does not become too frayed and break, you reel the fish close and glimpse your prize deep under the boat. The fish also sees the hull, gets scared and gets its final spurt of energy and dives deeper under the boat. By that time both you and the fish are exhausted. If you are lucky you reel it in the final few most difficult feet, shout "gaff" and one of the deck hands gaffs it, hoists it aboard and tags it with your number. It is then immediately flash frozen in the boat's hold. That exhilarating workout lasts from 15-45 minutes or longer depending on the size of the fish and is repeated many times throughout the day.

All fishermen strive to catch the biggest and most fish, in that order. That weekend, I caught a 74.8 lb. blue fin tuna and a total of more than 700 lbs. of fish, a record for me on both counts. That justified the purchase of a freezer to store the fish. It was the closest thing to fishing paradise.

That first trip convinced me to repeat it for the next few years. Matthew usually joined me and it was a wonderful bonding experience. One year, Shawn and Dale, my sons-in-law, joined us. The four of us caught 2200 lbs of tuna in one three-day trip. Several were exchanged for tuna fish cans; others were filleted or made into teriyaki tuna jerky.

Matt

Myself, son Matt, sons-in-law Shawn and Dale

Kodak Career

Early in my Kodak career, I had decided to abandon any medical school aspirations and focus on enhancing my position at Kodak. This was a very easy decision because I truly enjoyed my work and colleagues and had increasing financial responsibilities. I was fortunate to have a job that I could develop into a life-long career.

I will highlight some of my more interesting projects and document the changes that occurred from the halcyon days of the mid-sixties to the slow and painful transition to the digital age and the eventual downsizing of a corporate giant. Please remember that this is my perspective. I hope that in the end you will have a better appreciation of my world at Kodak.

At the time I joined Kodak in the fall of 1967, the company was the premier place to work in the Rochester area. It was by far the city's largest company, employing about ten percent of Rochester's population. Kodak comprised several "campuses" around the city. The three primary ones were Kodak Office (KO) in downtown Rochester, which housed the corporate offices; Kodak Apparatus Division (KAD) was a large camera and projector manufacturing division and was located across the Genesee River from Kodak Office. The third was Kodak Park (KP), a city within a city, located a few miles north of Kodak Office and where photographic film and paper were manufactured.

KP was a huge 1200 acre complex with its own railroad, fire department, streets and bus system. It had its own sewer and power generating system; indoor and outdoor sports complexes, bowling alleys, many libraries, several theaters, as well as many restaurants and stores selling everything from photographic equipment to safety shoes. Kodak had a large medical department with at least five full time physicians, several nurses, optometrists and hearing specialists.

I suspect most Fortune 500 companies had similar facilities at the time. What made Kodak unique were the many windowless buildings around Kodak Park necessitated by the light sensitive photographic film and paper. These buildings housed the huge emulsion coating machines (which were essentially large buildings) mounted on giant springs and shock absorbers to minimize any movement caused by passing trains or trucks. Film is composed of several layers of chemicals coated evenly on top of an optically pure plastic film base. Machines coated 54-

inch wide film sheets at more than 400 feet a minute, so the slightest vibrations caused ripples making the resulting film useless. Windowless buildings also housed film slitters, perforators, paper coatings and emulsion mixers. Although windowless, these buildings were tastefully designed with curved or triangular red brick walls and were intermingled with other typical buildings giving an overall pleasant atmosphere. It is rumored that during hot summer days, female employees in the windowless buildings worked in their underwear and provided an exciting diversion to supervisors equipped with night vision goggles

The recreational building known as Bldg 28 housed a state of the art 1900+ seat theater; a gymnasium with basketball, tennis and volley ball courts; a multi-lane bowling alley and it even housed a target shooting gallery. There were sanctioned bridge and euchre tournaments, tennis, volleyball, basketball and baseball leagues. First run movies for employees and their families were shown regularly and excursions to surrounding sporting events or ski resorts were always available.

I took advantage of many of the offered activities at various times during my tenure at Kodak. I played tennis or bridge at lunchtimes, joined some evening euchre tournaments and played volleyball on the research lab's team on Wednesday nights. I also joined golf and bowling leagues on Saturday and Thursday nights. We sometimes had lunch in the executive dining room. One of my favorite memories was going there on Tuesdays when the chef prepared his signature "liver and onions meal". I never liked liver but his was out of this world. I made it a point to commend him and asked for his recipe. He gave it to me and I prepared it at home. It tasted great but was such a mess to make; I was satisfied just having it at Kodak once a week.

Kodak Theater

One would think that all these activities were a little over the top. We spent a lot of time with our coworkers not only during work hours, but also during much of our discretionary time. The added value was unmistakable. Those of us who took advantage of these activities found ourselves truly enjoying the camaraderie, both at work and at play. We formed very strong respectful friendships, which lasted throughout our lifetimes.

The Kodak Research Laboratories were originally located in an ancient building very close to George Eastman 's original headquarters in the southeast area of Kodak Park. A few months after I joined the company, we moved into a brand new state-of-the-art research complex known as Buildings 81/82. In those days our directors boasted that the company was spending about one million dollars a day on research. We were growing at a rate slightly higher than the US Gross Domestic Product. We extrapolated that if we continued to grow at that rate, we would eventually be bigger than the US' GDP. What a foolish thought in light of the unforeseen digital transformation.

I started at Kodak in a very small electrochemical laboratory in the Analytical Sciences Division. Our group leader, Robert Large, was a Ph.D. chemist with a music undergraduate degree and a gregarious personality. The group was composed of John Stout, Carol Petrosky, Cecille Shorter, and myself. Jack Chang joined our lab shortly after I did. Like employees everywhere, you most often build the closest relationships with the people you begin working with and we were no exception.

Shortly after we moved into the new research complex, Bob Large was promoted and Jack Chang, in spite of his short tenure, was promoted to group leader. Jack was a very hard worker who respected his supervisors. It was amazing how quickly he mastered corporate politics and succeeded without sacrificing his ethics.   He eventually became one of the company's vice presidents responsible for the entire corporate research laboratories.   I'm introducing Jack in a little more detail because he was my first boss and I was his first group member. We worked very closely together on the same research projects and established a mutually respectful relationship.   He became my mentor and had a great effect on my behavior throughout the rest of my Kodak career.

Within a few months, the research labs were re-organized and Jack was named laboratory head of the newly formed Special Projects Laboratory. It was the "prestige" lab of our division. We worked on many unique and interesting projects, whereas the other units specialized in specific analytical procedures as a service to other divisions' projects.

As our lab grew, more people with different kinds of expertise were added.   Frank Lovecchio, Alex Wernberg, Norma Platt and Richard Dunlap as well as a few others joined in quick succession. This group formed the core of the Special Projects Laboratory and we remained lifelong friends, having lunch together, vacationing together and going out with our spouses as a group.

Early on in our careers, a memory expert, who used to work with the Washington Redskins, taught a memory course to the Kodak research labs scientists.

It was an evening class and we each paid $150 out of pocket to attend. Eager to improve our work performance, Frank, Jack, Alex, Norma, Richard and I decided to take it. The instructor boasted that by using his techniques, we would, by the end of the class, be able to memorize a fifty-digit number and recite it backwards on demand. He taught us a simple technique to do so. After finishing the class, my brother-in-law gave me a 50-digit number and saved it in his wallet. Six months later, he found the paper and asked me to recite it. I did and as soon as he told me to forget it, it was erased from my memory forever. So the class worked as advertised but no one really needs to remember fifty numbers in everyday life.

He also assured us that we would easily remember names and associate them with faces. The technique was to focus on a person's face, identify the most prominent characteristic and formulate an image associating the person's name with that characteristic. To demonstrate that, the instructor asked Ken O'Lone (a skeptical fellow student) to go to the front of the class and asked us to identify Ken's most prominent feature. It was his deep-set eyes. The instructor asked us to imagine two beer cans in Ken's eyes and a lawn curtain hanging from the cans covering Ken. The more bizarre the picture, the more memorable it is. To this day, I can see "cans-of-lawn" (which is phonetically close to "Ken O'Lone") in my mind's eye. Bob Moore had deep creases on the side of his cheeks. The imagery was to imagine <u>bob</u>cats jumping out of his creases, each pushing a lawn mower - Bob Moore. His system worked but making bizarre associations is sometimes more difficult than it seems.

Although remembering large numbers is useless and associating names with faces is cumbersome, he did however give us some useful suggestions I have used throughout my life. These include repeating someone's name once introduced. For example, as you shake hands, say, "Good to meet you, Rick Fox". Another useful technique concerns the problem of trying to remember to bring in an item at a later date. I usually envision a huge heavy book or whatever the item happens to be completely blocking the path to my car and I would have to physically remove it before proceeding. I know this technique works because I have often used it and rarely "forgotten" to bring anything I promised.

The early years at Kodak were a blur of learning new and exciting processes, meeting new people and getting acquainted with the corporate culture. We went through an induction period (just like in the service) when we were systematically exposed to safety procedures, signed non-disclosure documents and covered a myriad other details. Because photographic chemistry was not taught in colleges or universities, we attended many classes focused on the photographic process and culminated in graduating from "Color College". This was by no means the end of our training. There were many more training opportunities throughout the years covering many diverse topics such as speed-reading, problem solving, electrical engineering, management training seminars, sales and marketing courses, both in-house and at outside colleges and universities.

Please forgive me for subjecting you to a few boring photographic process details, but I think they are important so you can get a better appreciation of the various projects I was involved with and how serendipity played a significant role throughout my career.

The basic ingredient in any photographic film is silver. Silver is light sensitive and has the ability to spread when processed, making it the primary choice for traditional photographic systems. Silver however is only sensitive to ultraviolet light. That means it cannot "see" light in the visible spectrum. To help it "see", appropriate dyes are added to "sensitize" the silver. Three separate sensitizing dyes are generally used: cyan (for red sensitivity), magenta (for green sensitivity) and yellow (for blue sensitivity). These dyes, silver and other small amounts of various chemicals are mixed together with gelatin to form a thick slurry called an emulsion. Everything is then coated onto a transparent film base, dried, slit, perforated and packaged into light- tight containers.

When film is exposed to light, a few molecules of silver are formed in the exposed areas. These are so small they cannot be seen by the naked eye. Processing the film develops (i.e. amplifies) the silver in the image areas enough to make the image visible. Non-developed silver is then fixed (washed away). The film is washed of any excess chemicals and dried to make the exposed and processed negative.

The negative is then printed onto sensitized paper, which is processed to yield the finished pictures. Most of the silver coated in black and white film and ALL of the silver coated in color film is recovered and recycled. That is because in color film, silver development causes the visible dyes to form. Once the dye is formed, silver is no longer needed to visualize the image so it is bleached (re-oxidized), fixed (dissolved) and recovered.

At the time I joined Kodak, it was well known that three separate sensitizing dyes were needed to make film. Film builders had shelves full of these dyes and empirically tested several to obtain the optimum combinations. My first assignment was to understand how these dyes worked so we could take the guesswork out of the process and design more ideal compounds.

The first step in undertaking any research project was to do a thorough literature search on the topic. Nothing was computerized. One paper led to another. That initial library search involved reading every shred of published data and generally lasted from one to six or more weeks. We digested everything possible before plotting our course and formulating a set of experiments. At that time, every researcher was given a bound black notebook to document every experimental design, every note and every thought in ink. If anything needed changing, we neatly crossed out the old and added the new. Notebook entries had to be signed and dated by the researcher and witnessed by a colleague. In my tenure in research, I filled about one notebook a year. Imagine two thousand people in research, each filling one notebook a year!! No wonder Kodak hired an army of lawyers to painstakingly pour over a tremendous number of notebooks for the Polaroid instant camera litigation.

That first assignment started as a joint project with Jack Chang. He was promoted and I continued with the research on my own but he remained involved and provided valuable input whenever it was needed. It was six long years before we understood the mechanism of spectral sensitization well enough to present and publish our findings and several new dyes were designed based on our research. The many frustrating days with little or no progress were intermingled with a few days of significant breakthroughs, but these were sufficient to maintain our interest.

The next two or three years were spent on several exotic projects, only two of which are worth mentioning. The first project was related to our newly acquired computer. It was DEC PDP-11/05. My responsibility was to learn the "C" programming language and program the computer to calculate reaction kinetics. The computer was large enough to fill a room, had no keyboard and its front panel contained a series of toggle switches and blinking red lights. The information was fed into it using an integrated punched tape reader.

Programming the computer was tedious at best. I wrote the program (set of instructions) one line at a time then keypunched it onto a series of cards, one card per line of instruction. It was catastrophic to drop or mix the cards up. The cards were then fed through a mainframe computer, which compiled the program on a large, folded, perforated paper printout and a punched tape. The final step was to feed that punched tape into the PDP-11 computer. The program <u>never</u> worked the first time, so it was debugged by painstakingly going through every instruction on the printout to find and correct sequence, syntax or spelling errors. The entire process was then repeated until the program ran as expected. It may sound frustrating but I was so excited about this assignment that I used to come in on weekends and evenings to debug and retry the programs. I envisioned it as a challenging puzzle. We were able to use the computer to solve first and second order kinetic reactions. That experience probably influenced my lifelong fascination with computers.

The second project worth mentioning was investigating the merits of "heat processing". Exposed filmstrips were subjected to high temperatures circumventing the need for the messy wet processes. The process was intended for use in banks and other financial institutions to photograph and document cancelled checks. Although we proved feasibility, the project was not commercialized.

When I had been at the research labs about eleven years I realized that, although the projects were interesting and challenging, I was beginning to approach each new assignment in the same manner. I was starting to get a little antsy. I took stock of my situation, where I had been, where I was and where I was going. I was ready for a change. I reasoned that although I was doing well, I did not have a PhD and had to compete with many who did. This probably put me at a slight disadvantage in term of future promotions and I discussed this dilemma with our division head.

He assured me that I had proven that I could compete with the best of them as reflected in my increasing pay grade and indicated that I had a bright future in research. He reminded me that the research labs operated under a "dual ladder system", meaning one could choose the management or the research route and make the same amount of money. When I pressed him as to whether I had the same chance for advancement in management as a similar person equipped with a PhD, he admitted he would choose the person with the doctorate because he would be more respected by his staff. I was not comfortable knowing that my progress might be limited by any reason other than performance.

About that same time I happened to read Gail Sheehy's book Passages. It was the defining book on the passage of adults through life and I recommend it to anyone between the ages of twenty-five and fifty-five. I was thirty-six and her description fit me perfectly. Sheehy indicated that people in their mid-thirties generally pause to reflect on their careers. Some decide to continue on their path, some make minor adjustments, while others make big changes. Some even change professions. She also suggested that whatever decision a person made, most were eventually happy with their choices. This encouraged me to make a change although I was not sure what it was going to be. I just knew I wanted to stay at Kodak.

It was rare for anyone to leave the hallowed halls of research voluntarily, so there was a negative stigma for anyone transferring out. I was more interested in finding the right fit than I was concerned about the negative stigma. I talked to my mentor, Jack Chang, about my intentions. He was surprised and told me I was not quite ready to move on. He discouraged me but did not stand in my way.

I put out feelers indicating I would be available provided it was the right opportunity. Within a short time I received an offer from the Photographic Technology Division to work in their Processing Chemistry Laboratory. The new division was organized along product lines and served as a liaison between marketing and research. The various product lines were paper, x-ray, Kodak-chrome and Ekta-chrome, black and white film, and motion picture products. The groups worked very closely with the corresponding marketing entities and solved many of the "field" or customer problems.

My first few weeks there were somewhat difficult. Jack was right. I didn't know anything about how our products worked. In fact, I did not even understand what was said in meetings. They talked in codes and I truly thought they were trying to "snow" me. I later discovered that every division uses different terminology to describe the same thing. This was by design because of the many sensitive issues discussed in open meetings.

Working in the Processing Chemistry unit brought me in contact with essentially all the product groups and we were instrumental in solving several challenging and high profile problems. Within a few months I was promoted to group leader.

A few months before I transferred to the new division, the environmental group had installed a unique ion exchange silver recovery system capable of extracting the silver from wash water solutions in the largest East Coast photo processor - District Photo in Washington, DC.

Ion exchange is essentially similar in principle to home water softening devices, fairly easy to install and operate. In essence, the wash water from processing machines is passed through a column loaded with ion exchange resin. The resin attracts and holds on to the silver going by. When the resin is full, i.e. its capacity to retain silver is exhausted, an appropriate solvent is passed through the column again to release the silver and regenerate the resin.

The system installed at District Photo had many problems. The expensive resin "clogged up" and had to be constantly replaced. The efficiency of silver recovery was far below expectations and Kodak's reputation was at stake. The situation had deteriorated to the point that Ray DeMoulin, the assistant division director who was overseeing the installation, was ready to pull the plug. DeMoulin, several others and myself had a lengthy two-day meeting in a locked room to address the issues.

After a few hours of heated discussion, the real issues began to surface. The devil was in the details. The project leader and his staff were engineers, not chemists. I suspected that the problem was caused by an adverse chemical reaction, causing metallic silver to form and clog the columns. I indicated to Ray that I needed to run a few more experiments before I would be comfortable making any recommendations. He facilitated acquiring the staff and equipment to expedite the process and asked me to report directly to him. Within a few weeks, experiments indicated that the resin chosen was not ideal. Silver metal was indeed forming and clogging the columns and the solutions used to strip the loaded columns were not optimized. I made the recommendations to Ray who promptly named me project manager and I spent the next few months commuting between Rochester and Washington D.C. to implement the changes at the customer's facility.

The timing was perfect. We completed the project at the time the price of silver was at its peak. The Hunt brothers had temporarily cornered the silver market and in a short time the price of silver sky rocketed from about $6 troy oz. to more than $100 troy oz. The processing labs made significantly more money recovering silver from their processes than they did developing and printing film. At the conclusion of the project, I wrote and published a paper on the recovery of silver from dilute wash water solutions and presented it at the Photo Marketing Association (PMA) convention in Las Vegas that year.

This was just the beginning, because in Las Vegas I was asked by one of Kodak's managers to make that same presentation to the major motion picture laboratories in Hollywood. At that time, there were three main Hollywood motion picture laboratories, Technicolor, MGM and Deluxe and the competition between them was fierce. Technicolor and Deluxe were already recovering their wash water silver with various degrees of success but MGM was not.

Once MGM heard my presentations, they were anxious to have a similar system installed at their facility. That necessitated my frequent travels to Hollywood to design and install the MGM system, which was larger and much more complicated than the one at District Photo. The system worked flawlessly for many years and recovered its total cost in less than six months.

My many trips to Hollywood exposed me to the Hollywood office personnel and many of our customers. We established a mutually beneficial relationship, because a few months later, they needed a technical person and asked me to consider transferring to the motion picture division and relocating to Hollywood.

This was a big decision! Barbara was happy teaching elementary school in Irondequoit (Rochester suburb) and we enjoyed the many friends and relatives around us. We had just moved into our new house and life was good. On the other hand, Jessica and Matthew were six and four years old, so a move would not disrupt their young lives too much. Barbara is sometimes resistant to change, so I approached the subject very delicately. To my surprise she didn't reject the idea. Ray DeMoulin also invited Barbara and me to his house for dinner one evening to convince her that this assignment would enhance my career. He assured us that we could return in four to five years and he would hold my position open in Rochester in case we wanted to come home sooner. That persuaded her to look at the move as an opportunity and we began to make preparation for our move to California.

Kodak made our move completely painless. They bought our house at its market value and paid all moving expenses including packing and unpacking EVERYTHING. They moved our plants, cars and even unused firewood. Once we moved they gave us a $5000 "curtain" allowance (yes, for drapes and curtains) as well as a monthly allowance to defray the cost of the higher California mortgage.

Many Kodak colleagues who came from Rochester before us chose Thousand Oaks because it was very similar to the environment we left in Rochester. Thousand Oaks, named for its thousand California Oak trees, had quiet streets and good schools. We appreciated the built-in support group who helped us settle into our new environment. Our California house was the same size and age as the house we left in Rochester. It had a smaller yard but made up for that with a nice pool. In short, both houses were essentially equivalent. The only difference was the size of the mortgage. It doubled from $50,000 to $100,000.

Barbara decided not to teach the first year we were in California and the move to Hollywood was not associated with a pay increase. Despite the increased mortgage and the elimination of Barbara's salary, we seemed to be more comfortable financially than we were in Rochester. That was due to several factors. First, I received a company car and Kodak covered all its expenses including gas, maintenance and insurance. Second, California's property taxes were significantly lower than New York's, and finally, winter clothes were no longer necessary and this reduced our clothing budget. I'm sure there are other reasons I'm forgetting. The surprising end result was that we were better off financially even on one salary.

On the business end, I changed divisions again and underwent another rigorous training program to become a marketing person. To my surprise, I found that even in marketing they used different terminology than I had become accustomed to. It did not take long to understand and become fluent in their techno-speak.

Being the rookie in the Hollywood office, I was assigned to the least desirable customers, the ones whose survival had minimal impact on Kodak's bottom line. I did not mind because I enjoyed the new environment and was quickly picking up marketing skills.

That first year in marketing was exciting. It was fun meeting new customers, wining and dining, attending sports events including the Lakers NBA finals, Rose Bowl parade and game. I could not believe I was actually getting paid to have all that fun. Unfortunately all that entertaining coupled with quitting smoking caused me to gain about thirty pounds that first year.

I was forty-one years old at the time and my weight gain was not my only problem. My hair was always prematurely grey but now I was meeting many new people and figured that my graying hair may be a liability. One Sunday night I went to the store, bought black hair dye and applied it. Barb was out and I wanted to surprise her with a younger looking version of myself. When she returned, she looked at me and burst out laughing. She said it looked like I had applied jet-black shoe polish to my head and that I could not be seen like this. I didn't realize my hair should be anything but black so I suggested I strip the dye using peroxide and re-dye it with a dark shade of brown. It was Sunday night and the stores were closed so I had to wait until the next morning. Barb agreed to stay home the next day to work on my problem. As soon as the drug store opened, we purchased hydrogen peroxide and a more natural shade of brown hair dye. Once bleached and re-dyed, my hair looked even worse than before. It turned "orangutan orange". Now I was in a worse predicament. I had to go to work because our newly appointed national marketing director was in Hollywood and wanted to meet with all of his staff. I had no alternative but to wear a hat and go to the office. The only way to justify my tardiness was to take my hat off and share my saga. Word spread like wildfire to all parts of the globe as well as to our local customers. Later attempts to fix the problem improved the color but subsequent bleaching by the sun changed it to various shades of green and magenta. Customers and worldwide colleagues continued to laugh at my expense to the end of my Kodak career.

That first year in Hollywood brought us another totally unexpected benefit. One of my more enterprising colleagues proposed that Kodak provide Princess Cruise lines with photographic guest lecturers. In return, the cruise company would provide a stateroom for the lecturer and spouse as well as airfare to and from the embarkation and destination points. The proposal was accepted and one of the Hollywood office team was privileged to become a guest lecturer on one or more cruises. This was not a "Kodak sanctioned endeavor". It was a group of guys from different backgrounds who worked at Kodak's Hollywood Motion Picture office. I was not an expert photographer but my enterprising colleague had put together a series of three or four lectures, provided scripts and slide shows, hand-out literature and a kit with extra cameras and batteries in case any of the passengers needed help with their cameras. In other words everything was provided to make any of us look and sound like experts. We lectured (Barbara assisted by operating the projector and handing out the literature) on three cruises, two to Alaska and one through the Panama Canal. We were treated like minor celebrities, able to enjoy all the ship's amenities and only lectured on sea days, which generally amounted to three or four lectures for each cruise. It was a great experience.

After my first year at Hollywood, I was assigned to more critical customers, finally becoming the account executive for Technicolor. At the time I dealt with them, they were one of the Kodak's largest customers. They were arrogant and had to be dealt with honestly and tactfully. They were challenging at best.

On one occasion, Kodak introduced a new faster and more sensitive negative film to the industry. Technicolor and some of their customers (the studios) noticed a moon-shaped fog on the processed negative. The Kodak account executive responsible for Paramount told the studio that it was a Technicolor problem and Technicolor blamed the problem on Kodak's new film. Finger pointing is not unusual for Hollywood as it is everywhere else. Technicolor's president, Ron Jarvis, was livid and banned the Paramount representative from ever stepping inside Technicolor. Jarvis stated to me that he would never admit to a negative problem being their fault, regardless of whose fault it really was, because their reputation rested on their negative processes.

Although other labs were experiencing problems with the new negative, none were the same as the crescent shaped fog seen at Technicolor. I wanted to observe how their film was handled. They only process film at night so I went into the lab about midnight and followed a few rolls of film from the time they arrived to the laboratory until they came out of the processing machine. The first step was to wind the incoming film onto another reel (in the dark) and feel the film by cupping it between the thumb and index finger to make sure there were no torn perforations. Torn perforations weakened the film causing it to break in the processing machine and that would be catastrophic.

I knew the new film was more sensitive to pressure than its predecessor, so I thought the film occasionally rubbed on the operator's ring causing the fog but trying it in our laboratory failed to reproduce the problem. I tried cupping the film with differing amounts of pressure and discovered that increased cupping pressure reproduced the problem. Now, how do I approach Jarvis with that news? I decided to meet him and his vice president in person. I went to his office at the appointed time and they were both waiting for me. I closed the door and bluntly told them that they were the cause of the fogging crescents and therefore they were the only ones who could resolve the issue. I informed them that although the new film was more sensitive than the old, other laboratories were not experiencing that problem. I suggested that one or more of their operators were cupping the film a little more severely than they should. I emphasized that these operators were being conscientious, not unduly rough and should be trained to handle the film more gingerly rather than be punished for any wrongdoing. Before I left, I assured them that I understood the sensitivity of this issue and I was not going to share this episode with anyone in Hollywood.

The problem "mysteriously" disappeared shortly afterwards and I did not hear another word about this issue for a long time. A few years later, I left Kodak and went to work for Technicolor. Jarvis reminded me of the time I was gutsy enough to walk into his office to tell him HE had a problem. It is probably the one incident in which I gained his respect.

Although assigned to work in the Hollywood office, one of the international managers from headquarters wanted me (specifically) to evaluate a laboratory in Sao Paulo, Brazil for possible acquisition by Kodak. This was highly unusual but I relished the adventure of going to Brazil and the break from my daily routines.

This was my first international trip on Kodak's behalf. In those days Kodak's policy permitted first class travel for all international flights. Airlines truly pampered first class passengers and our flights were so lavish we hated to reach our destination.

We flew into Rio de Janeiro, where I had the added responsibility of demonstrating our newly introduced color negative film to about 150 Directors of Cinematography. The sound was a little low so I motioned to the projectionist to increase the volume. When the sound was just right I indicated that it was OK by the usual thumb to index finger gesture. To my surprise, the audience roared with laughter. That was because our A-OK sign is equivalent to giving someone the "bird" in Brazil. It was embarrassing but interesting to know that hand gestures can vary that widely around the world.

Rio de Janeiro is one of the most beautiful cities in the world and its many beaches, with their white sand and healthy girls in their string bikinis were more beautiful than we expected. The restaurants are great. Their specialty is churrasco (a Brazilian counterpart of barbecue), a meal of grilled meats on over-sized skewers. Feijoada (a black bean and meat stew, made from leftovers) is popular especially for Wednesday and Saturday lunch. Local people from Rio are referred to as Cariocas. You don't have to be born in Rio to be a Carioca. All you have to do is relax into the city lifestyle and soon you will become one.

Nightlife is filled with dance clubs and discos catering to every taste. On the spicier side Rio has more than its share of nightclubs featuring nude dancers and erotic performances. Our Brazilian guide suggested we visit one of them and took us there in spite of our vehement "protests"!! I have never seen anything like it and probably never will again. It was OVER THE TOP! The first thing you notice on entering the nightclub are the white leather couches scattered around three or four small stages and dozens of beautiful girls milling around the guys sitting on the couches. On a scale of 1-10, all the girls were eights and above. As soon as we chose our seats, several of them offered us drinks and hung around to talk. My colleague took a liking to one of them who happened to be from Lebanon and spoke Arabic. I told her that my friend liked her. Within minutes she was sitting next to him, rubbing his chest and legs and getting his drinks. My "poor" conservative, bland, Midwestern friend thoroughly enjoyed the experience. While this is going on, the milling girls got on one of the stages, stripped and danced to the blaring music. Shortly after we got there, the lights dimmed and two girls and a guy got on stage, started to disrobe and began to have live sex. The tension at the club was palpable! As the guy approached orgasm, the whole crowd got quiet and the music volume decreased in anticipation of the big event! As soon as the desired effect was reached all the girls as well as many customers applauded and the music reflected their mood. It was almost comical and, as far as I was concerned, not the least bit erotic. It was definitely a unique way to be introduced to Brazil.

The next morning we flew to Sao Paulo in a rickety Varig jet for the business part of our trip. Curt é Alex Laboratory in Sao Paulo was using our products but owed Kodak a significant amount of money and was having trouble paying their bills. Meanwhile, Leader laboratory, their main competitor was doing well and was subsidized by our competitor, Agfa. Kodak's market share was beginning to decline. After a thorough investigation and several trips to Brazil, I determined that the lab was on sound footing because they had several significant customers, good modern machines and a knowledgeable staff. I recommended we go ahead with the acquisition, which we did. We managed to increase our market share and witnessed the demise of Leader laboratories. Ironically, a few years later, Kodak was interested in selling that lab and Technicolor was interested in expanding into South America. By that time I was working at Technicolor so Jarvis asked me to go to Brazil to re-evaluate Curt é Alex and another lab in Buenos Aires, Argentina. Unfortunately we could not agree on price but the exercise was fun and exposed me to many international customers.

Not long after that I was promoted again to Director of Engineering of the motion picture division for the entire western US & Canada. It was a fun job with varied responsibilities. These included being the liaison between Kodak in Rochester and our customers. This was not as exciting as it seems because, in reality, I was the customer's advocate with Kodak and Kodak's advocate with customers.... always a somewhat adversarial position. Other responsibilities included being Kodak's representative to various societies and organizations. I served on the board of directors of the Society of Motion Picture and Television Engineers (SMPTE), joined the American Society of Cinematographers (ASC), the Motion Picture Academy of Arts and Sciences and the Television Academy. It was an honor to be invited to these prestigious organizations.

In the early 90's, Ted Turner surprised the motion picture world by acquiring the MGM library. He did it to keep his newly formed cable network supplied with classic movies. At that same time, DVDs were just beginning to proliferate and the sudden interest in old movies exploded. The studios discovered that they were sitting on gold mines and dusted off their old films for repurposing in those newly emerging ancillary markets. Unfortunately, old movies were beginning to deteriorate because most were stored in less than ideal conditions.

I initiated a series of seminars for studio heads and their designees on dye stability, film preservation and film restoration. This proved mutually beneficial to the studios, Kodak and myself personally. I consulted with Warner Brothers and Paramount in building their state-of-the-art vaults. The studios were able to save their deteriorating assets, Kodak benefited from their value added good will and I emerged as one of Hollywood's primary experts on film preservation and restoration.

As director of engineering, I came across a lot of interesting facts about film worth sharing, some trivial, others not so. Here are a few of them:

- Movie film runs at 24 frames a second. So, a professional 35mm movie camera takes the same number of pictures as on a twenty-four exposure roll of amateur film – every second.

- Imax runs 65 mm negatives at 60 frames a second. If an Imax film ran the same amount of time as a typical 35 mm movie, it would be more than 80,000 feet long and weigh a ton. Studies show that 24 frames per second is ideal information for the brain to comfortably absorb so a longer Imax movie would exhaust viewers.

- A typical movie is one hour and fifty minutes, which is about 10,000 feet of film. It is delivered to the movie theaters in five or six containers, each holding up to 2,000 feet of film. The reels are then spliced together by the projectionists. Trailers are spliced on to the front end. When the film has finished playing that theatre, the movie is un-spliced, put back in the cans, and then sent to another theatre.

- The size of a typical screen in a typical multi-plex is 40- to 60-feet wide. To project a 35mm film image on that screen, the image must be enlarged about 600 times.

- Movies are shot on color negative film – and shown on color print film. Because of fear of damaging the original negative, movies are printed from 'internegatives'. The total amount of film used in a large Hollywood blockbuster, in wide release, would be enough to almost go around the equator and cost the studio more than six million dollars. That is less than one percent of the film's total budget.

- A typical movie print costs the studio less than $1000 and is shown 300 times. That means that print cost is about $3 per showing – so the first person purchasing a ticket for each showing more than pays for the cost of the movie print.

- More than three billion feet of movie print film is accounted for, destroyed and recycled annually.

- And finally, it takes the gelatin of about fifty cows to manufacture the film for a typical movie.

These points are quickly becoming obsolete because movie studios and theater owners are undergoing a massive transition to the digital world.

One of my proudest achievements was my role in acquiring two Oscar statuettes for Kodak. This involved submitting a comprehensive application justifying the merits of each invention, making demonstrations and presentations to the academy members and finally negotiating the politics of the Technical Awards Committee to convince them of the compliance of the specific innovation to the many academy guidelines.

George Fisher, Kodak's then CEO flew in to receive the Oscar on behalf of Kodak. He met me at the pre-awards party and asked me what I did for Kodak. I informed him that I was the guy who did all the preliminary work, which earned the award for which he was receiving all the glory. He just smirked and said "Oh well" and that was the last I heard from him.

In the early nineties the company began to feel the impact of the increasing competition from Fuji and the encroachment of digital imaging. We tried to reinvent ourselves. We dabbled in new businesses such as pharmaceuticals and copiers. We tried "half heartedly" to delve into the digital domain while maintaining our film business but could not compete. We even got into the videotape business for a short time to no avail. It seems we were in a quagmire and could not find a way out. We were also bloated with personnel. That's when a series of reduction in force (RIFS) programs began to take effect. The nineties decade brought a significant amount of retirements and layoffs. A huge number of people in the fifty to sixty age groups were downsized. I walked in one of the large Kodak Office buildings one day and saw nothing except rugs from wall to wall. No partitions, desks, chairs or equipment on floor after floor. This was a very eerie and disconcerting feeling.

1997 was not a good year for me for two reasons. First, my father's chronic leukemia flared up and he did not want to go through chemo- or radiation therapy. I could see that he was nearing the end. Second, I suspected I would be laid off. I was lucky enough to be able to choose a project that required my presence in Rochester. I spent his last couple of months at his bedside and he passed away peacefully that fall.

Sure enough, a couple of months later, I was offered a golden parachute if I chose to retire before the end of that year. I left Kodak in the fall of 1997 at the age of fifty-five. I was one of the fortunate few who received essentially all of my retirement benefits and an enhanced severance package. Luckily I had established a good rapport with our customers and as mentioned earlier, started working for Technicolor.

As I looked back on my tenure at Kodak, I saw a huge difference between the Kodak I joined in 1967 and the company I left in 1997.

From the beginning, Kodak was vertically integrated. This means that Kodak manufactured everything it needed to make its products. The company made the raw chemicals to combine into the emulsions; the paper for prints and packaging, the film cans from raw steel and the polymers to make the various film bases, etc.   Essentially nothing was outsourced, with the exception of gelatin. Even the building construction firm was a wholly owned subsidiary.   This insured tight quality controls in every stage along the production chain.

In the late 1920's Kodak encountered a severe film-fogging problem that was isolated to a batch of gelatin obtained from the Peabody Massachusetts Gelatin Company (PMGC). The gelatin contained an excess amount of sulfur and originated from a herd of cows, which ate a high level of mustard weeds and known to contain sulfur. Controlling the quality of the gelatin was essential so Kodak acquired the Peabody Company, cows, pastures, slaughterhouse and all.

The bulk of Kodak's earnings were derived from the consumable film rather than from cameras and projectors. Although Kodak made, serviced and sold anything related to the photographic industry, it was the film that was the lifeblood of the company and film was very difficult to make. It required the right combination of science and art. The general emulsion ingredients are determined by the science but every emulsion needed final tweaking by the addition of several addenda by very highly experienced and paid emulsion "doctors". This fact and the extremely high cost of "getting into the business" protected us from the encroachment of competitors and allowed the large profit margins we enjoyed.

The company valued its employees as reflected by the pay scales. Because of the very specialized nature of the business, Kodak spent a large amount of time training and developing its workers. As a result hardly anyone left the company voluntarily. There were no unions and our pay was equal to or more than the corresponding union wages. Every March the company distributed a wage dividend ranging from 10% to 15% of an individuals pay and was based on the previous years company profits. The individual had the choice of receiving the dividend as a lump sum or depositing it into a retirement account with deferred income taxes. This was in addition to the regular 401K programs where the company matched an individual's contributions to the allowable limits.

Most promotions came from within. This worked well in a stable environment but left the company vulnerable as we transitioned to digital photography. Company executives were exceptional in running the stable traditional business but were clueless in the new world of product lines with a few months' life span.

About the early eighties two factors came into play which had a major effect on the Kodak's bottom line. At that time Kodak enjoyed an 80-90% market share. A few years later, sleepy little Fuji Film Company began to wake up! They built a film manufacturing company in the US and began to significantly undercut Kodak's prices. Their film was not quite as good but it improved in time and they started to gain more market share.

The second factor was the encroachment of digital technology into the photographic arena. Kodak had expertise in camera manufacturing and optics and owned several sensor technology patents. It was ready to reinvent itself into a digital company but needed an army of electrical and electronic engineers. Kodak identified the most promising young people and sent them to universities to gain the required expertise. The company also hired brand new graduates in the required disciplines.

Many years later it was proven that we really could not or would not be big players in the digital domain. Our market share steadily decreased requiring an associated decrease in personnel. More "bean counters" were brought in to stabilize the bottom line. They cut services and outsourced anything possible thereby exacerbating the problems. For the first time in its 115-year history, an outsider, George Fisher replaced the Kodak-bred CEO. Kodak executives from the old school surrounded Fisher and they could not turn the company around.

Kodak's worldwide employees dwindled from a high of greater than 130,000 to about 16,000. Many of Kodak Park's buildings were demolished and the ones remaining were leased out to independent companies. In my short 30 years there, Kodak went from a robust leader of the photographic business to a small player in that market, a fate impossible to predict in the mid sixties.

My transition from Kodak to Technicolor was interesting at best. The corporate culture at Technicolor was different. Disagreements were handled directly and forgotten, whereas in the refined Kodak system, disagreements were subtle and festered for years. Technicolor was much smaller and moved much faster. The engineering director at the time I was hired was falling out of favor and I suspect I was hired as a potential replacement, although I was not specifically told so.

After solving a few technical problems, getting accustomed to their culture and earning my stripes, Ron Jarvis, Technicolor's president, asked me if I would be willing to start and run a new company to restore old films. Start-up costs were minimal because Technicolor owned many surplus printers and space was available. Wet film developing was contracted to the parent Technicolor and union contracts were renegotiated to achieve more favorable terms.

We grew into a five-million-dollar company with a significant profit margin within the first year, far exceeding our expectation. Unfortunately, that phenomenal success was not enough to guarantee my continued employment. A young, non-industry bean counter from MCI replaced Ron Jarvis and many of Ron's top managers left Technicolor shortly afterwards, including myself.

I was not quite ready to retire, so decided to investigate two different options. The first was to purchase an existing film restoration laboratory whose President and founder was ready to retire. The second was to start a film preservation and restoration consulting business aimed at Hollywood's largest studios.

My timing was perfect, because as soon as Paramount Studios heard that I was available, they expressed an interest in talking to me. Paramount had just purchased the rights to the library containing most of John Wayne's films and needed a person to identify the quality of the library as well as restore the deteriorating films. I was not ready to commit to full time employment because I was very interested in pursuing my other option. I suggested a high hourly rate, expecting to work ten to twenty hours a week. They accepted my proposal immediately.

I concurrently retained an attorney and an accountant and started the due diligence process on acquiring the new lab. Within six months, we started earnest price negotiations and discovered that their expectations and ours were too far apart. The film restoration business had limited growth potential, the field was getting crowded with several small competing labs, and I did not want to work 24/7 for the foreseeable future. We aborted the acquisition plan and I focused my attention on consulting for the studios.

My initial project at Paramount was winding down but before it was completed I was given another assignment managing their film assets vaulted around the globe. One project led to another and I continued consulting for Paramount full time for the following few years. It was the most lucrative, stress-free and fun period of my working life. It was also an ideal way to ease into retirement.

A little over five years from the time I started consulting for Paramount, their film and television divisions were reorganized, new players appeared and my projects began to dwindle. I was sixty-four years old and wanted to devote full time to the design and building of our new house in Temecula. I retired and entered utopia.

Utopia

Def. n. A place or state of great happiness

A few years before we retired, Barbara and I began to consider whether to retire in Thousand Oaks, move back to Rochester with our friends and relatives, move to Temecula where Dianne and Jessica lived with their families, or move to a city like Pasadena or San Diego with their many cultural activities. Thousand Oaks was eliminated because our kids had moved out and it was too far from any of our LA friends. Rochester was rejected for several reasons but primarily because of the severe winters.   The remaining options were Pasadena/San Diego or Temecula.

Temecula is a charming small city of about 100,000 people, located approximately 25 miles east of Oceanside, California. It is almost equidistant to San Diego, Los Angeles and Orange County. Temecula is the only city in California to still retain its original Indian name, meaning "the Place of the Sun". Eastern Temecula is known as the wine capital of Southern California with over two-dozen wineries and more than 3,500 acres of producing vineyards. The mountainous region west of the city is known for

its avocado and citrus orchards. The city boasts
Pechanga Indian Resort and Casino, the largest
Indian gaming complex west of the Mississippi. "Old
Town Temecula" is a collection of historic 1890s
buildings, hotels, specialty food stores, boutiques, gift
and collectible stores and antique dealers. It features
car shows, western days and summer entertainment. A
Temecula Valley Balloon and Wine Festival is held
annually at neighboring Lake Skinner and attracts
thousands of people from throughout California.

San Diego and Pasadena on the other hand are
vibrant cities, well known for their excellent weather
and many universities with their associated cultural
centers. They are also famous for their world-class
restaurants, theaters and museums.

We resolved our dilemma by asking the question
"What makes us happiest?" It was obvious that our
happiest times were spent being with Dianne, Jessica,
Matthew and their families. Our plan was to move to
Temecula as soon as we retired while Jessica's kids
were young and eventually move to San Diego or
Pasadena.

While visiting one Sunday in August of 2002, we
discussed our plan with Dianne and Jessica. As a
child I loved going to Giddo and Taita's (Grandpa &
Grandma's in Arabic) house every week for dinner.
We envisioned buying some property and building a
house where Barbara and I were now the Giddo and

Taita. Everyone would come to dinner every Sunday like I used to do at my grandfather's house in Zeitoun. <u>Zeitoun To Temecula!!</u>

As soon as Dianne heard this, she looked in the Sunday paper for properties for sale. Before I knew it, she found a few and called one of the listing agents. That very afternoon he showed us a few properties in Temecula's wine country as well as in De Luz, which is located in the mountains just west of the freeway.

The third or fourth property we saw was a five-acre, unimproved, mountaintop lot in De Luz. It was fortunate the agent drove a four-wheel drive Jeep because he took us to the top of the property, where the view was breath taking. He obviously knew what he was doing because had he shown it to us from street level, we would have not given it another thought.

The minimum building lot size in De Luz was five acres. What were we going to do with five acres when we only needed a fraction of that size? The agent quickly told us that this was a prime avocado-growing region as evidenced by the many groves stretching as far as the eye could see. He suggested we plant an income-producing grove with the extra land and this was an appealing idea worth considering.

We looked at several other lots in the area but kept comparing them to that original one with the great views. We went back for another look and began thinking about all the steps and expense it would take to transform this raw land into the "Mina compound", a daunting task.

This property has several advantages. It is only a few minutes away from the center of town, yet felt serene and quiet. It lies outside the local homeowners association district obviating the need to pay annual fees and comply with extra rules and regulations. More importantly, the higher elevation and afternoon ocean breeze keep the ambient temperatures about ten degrees cooler than Temecula.

The agent sensed our interest and suggested we make a non-binding offer, rescindable within one or two days. He also advised us to go to the Riverside planning office to examine the specific lot building requirements.

We agreed and suspected that going through with the deal was remote at best. We made the offer late that afternoon and, before we knew it, the offer was accepted.

We had five years from the time our offer was accepted to the time Barb and I planned to retire. It took the whole five years to transform that plot of raw land into an avocado-yielding orchard with a nicely landscaped single story house.

The first step was to hire a civil engineer to design a grading plan. A grading plan specifies building pad location, grove layout including service roads, driveway location and slope, septic tank and leach line positions and finally storm water flow calculations, which specify V-shaped cement gutters, burms and runoff channels to minimize erosion. Although the grading plan was completed in a couple of months, the required approval consumed about eighteen months of our five-year window. That delay was not caused by any deficiency in the plan itself, but by the total incompetence of the planner responsible for its approval. I appealed my case up the chain of command to the department head before approval was granted and we embarked on the actual grading of the property.

Next, we installed a water meter and arranged for a farm management company to install the irrigation system and plant and mulch our young avocado trees. The three-foot sticks (trees) were planted in November 2003 and yielded our first avocados in Spring 2007.

Meanwhile, we had been designing our new house. We envisioned a not-so-big-house with separate guest quarters to accommodate our East coast fellow retired friends and relatives and a great room and large kitchen to enjoy our anticipated family Sunday dinners. We began with a white paper and drew circles that defined functional areas with our living quarters on one side and the guest wing opposite our area. A great room and kitchen separated the two sections. The design was gradually refined until Barbara and I were comfortable with it. We retained an architect to convert our design into building plans. I was not entirely satisfied with the architect's rendering because the plan lacked any unique ceiling and/or floor treatment needed to differentiate the functional areas of our fairly open floor plan. Up to this point we had been working with a local builder who recommended the architect and was present at many of our meetings. He too was not much help with the creative aspects of ceiling and floor designs. We were also getting close to submitting the plans for competitive bids and I asked the architect to recommend a few builders. He gave us some referrals and indicated one in particular, who built a good house but was a little pricey.

I made an appointment to see Jeff Brand, the supposedly expensive builder and went to see him at a house he was completing in Temecula. The new house owner was also there, seemed happy with her experience and recommended Jeff highly. He looked at our plan and immediately started making suggestions on improvements before I mentioned my concerns. It seemed he read my mind because most of his suggestions targeted the plan's weaknesses. I took him to the property to discuss the location of the house on the pad and gave him a copy of our grading and building plans so he could give us a preliminary cost estimate. I mentioned the architect's comment about his prices and he assured me that no one could beat his prices, house for house.

A week later we met again in his office and Barbara and I were totally impressed. It was a small one-room building with a bathroom located next to his modest house. It was neat, airy and had an interesting ceiling treatment. He also took us to see some of the houses he built in Fallbrook, which seemed to be well built and all his clients seemed to like and respect him. His initial estimate was within our budget, so we signed a preliminary contract.

He and I met a few more times and the final meeting lasted about eight hours. Barbara and I had been making notes, saving magazine ideas and hashing through various ideas on window treatments, kitchen and bathroom design and many other details. After sharing these with Jeff, he and I forged ahead adding arches, ceiling treatments and curved walls and counter tops for aesthetic appeal. We fed on each other's ideas and continued the synergy until we ended with a plan that Barbara and I were happy with. A year and a half after our initial meeting with Jeff, our house plans were completed and submitted to the county for plan check and approval. Jeff began getting actual bids from his subcontractors for the final budget.

In the meantime, I applied for a building loan. I chose this financing option because the bank ensured the proposed budget was within tight guidelines and "policed" the builder to ensure that funds were disbursed according to the approved budget.

Unfortunately, Jeff's final budget was about $250,000 higher than his preliminary budget and that resulted in some heated discussions. I decided to resubmit the plans to two other builders for bids. My banker, who also became a friend, was building a house at the same time. He confirmed that during our negotiating timeframe, building prices skyrocketed and Jeff's higher bid was not out of line. This was confirmed by the competitive bids, which were significantly higher than Jeff's.

We had a little trouble getting the plans approved, again due to the county's desire to prolong the process to "keep the meter running". They finally approved the plans in April of 2006.

The next step was to orient the house on the pad. I wanted to make sure we would have bright morning sunlight streaming into the breakfast nook area in the spring. Jeff and I placed the newly approved building plans on a table at 10 o'clock one morning and turned it around until the pencil shadow hit the right position. We proceeded to stake the outline of the house to define its orientation on the building pad.

We broke ground the next week and the real work began. Jeff had developed a detailed project timeline, which he shared with us and it was fun monitoring the building progress. He also provided us with a list of all the subcontractors and their phone numbers and indicated I was free to talk to them directly regarding any problems or concerns. I believe this "open" relationship streamlined the process and reduced the stress associated with building a house.

I took great satisfaction in watching the final phase of our dream become a reality. Of course we had a few problems and misunderstandings but all were resolved amicably.

In retrospect, I must have subconsciously understood the complexity of this undertaking because it took about five years from concept to reality. The sequence of events had to be precise and the project monitored carefully. A permit was required for each phase and each permit had an expiration date. Moreover, some phases could go on concurrently, whereas others could not start before the previous phase was completed. I developed a project timeline and stuck to it. All the planning paid off because, except for a few glitches, the project was completed just in time and close to budget. We literally moved into our new house the day after Barbara retired and a few days before we were required to move out of our old house.

We spent the next few months unpacking, hanging pictures, personalizing our work areas and doing the thousand other things to convert the new house into our home. This was a great way to transition from our busy work schedules into the more relaxing retirement phase.

Like most working people, we were a little concerned about what we were going to "do" during retirement and shared this with our son, Matt. He quickly replied that our life was going to be just like it was before we entered kindergarten, except that we were not going to need our parent's help and money. He was absolutely right.

As it turned out, our concern about transitioning into retirement was totally unnecessary!! We did not need to transition into "Utopia".

We are completely free to do essentially anything anytime we desire. We can go to sleep or wake up whenever our bodies dictate, we can associate with people we like and not have to deal with people we don't. Numbers like weight, age or even money lose their importance. Barbara and I are enjoying a totally stress-free life. It's true that small aches and pains are increasing, but these are an insignificant price to pay, at least at this time of our lives

I essentially spend my life playing. I play competitive bridge three or four times a week, play golf once a week, play poker with my old LA friends a few times a month and play with my grandchildren often. I also try to work out two or three times a week.

Duplicate Bridge has turned out to be a challenging and enjoyable activity. I've often said that learning to be a good bridge player is more difficult than attending graduate school. It is a game of guidelines and nuances, where exceptions are the norm. Respectable players must be able to recognize hand patterns, deduce the cards in their partners' and opponents' hands, exercise good judgment and most importantly, be disciplined. Bridge turned out to be an ideal retirement hobby. It provides the needed mental exercise in a neat social environment.

The goal of every beginning serious bridge player is to become a life master. This requires much time and effort because only 1st, 2nd and 3rd place winners earn fractional points at club and tournament events.

There are many American Contract Bridge League (ACBL) sanctioned clubs. Several local area clubs combine to form a section, several sections form a region, and several regions make up the nationals. To become a life master you must earn a minimum of 300 points. These must include at least fifty silver points which are awarded only at Sectional tournaments, fifty red and twenty five gold points which are awarded only at Regional tournaments. I recently became a life master and discovered it that is only the beginning. There are bronze, silver, gold, diamond and emerald life masters, with a handful of individuals topping the 50,000-point mark.

As an enjoyable working diversion from all that play, I also manage our avocado grove. I expected it to be an easy straightforward effort to maintain irrigation, fertilization and harvesting schedules. These turned out to be more challenging than anticipated because there are no exact recommendations and production yields are affected by many factors.

Irrigation is the most important because water is increasingly expensive and providing just the right amount to maintain optimum production is critical.

The right amount of water is dependent on many factors such as weather conditions, root depths, ground slope, soil type and several others. An average avocado tree requires about 200 gallons per week during the hot summer months. Providing more water leads to waste and runoff and less water stresses the tree and reduces yield. Optimum irrigation is therefore accomplished by frequent small volume watering schedules. But that presents other problems.

1. It is labor intensive and requires irrigators to turn the water on and off and walk the lines to inspect and repair the many frequent breaks and emitter clogs.

2. Salts tend to concentrate in the watering area and inhibit the tree's capacity to absorb the provided water. These salts must be leached out of the soil by periodic flushing with excess water.

3. Irrigation volumes are determined by current weather conditions but must be balanced to accommodate water allocation constraints.

I have devised an extremely efficient automatic irrigation system composed of a smart irrigation controller coupled to a separate grove water meter. The controller downloads daily satellite weather data and adjusts irrigation accordingly. Comparing the volumes allocated by the controller with actual water meter readings provides immediate feedback on breaks and/or blockages and obviates the need for manual inspections. This irrigation system has reduced our grove's water consumption about 30%, significantly reduced our labor costs and increased our yield. My son-in-law and I are commercializing this process and beginning to sign up customers.

Harvesting decisions are another non-trivial concern. Avocados don't ripen on the tree. The harvesting season starts in mid-February to early March when the avocado's oil content reaches marketability. The primary factors affecting that decision are price and size. Typically a grove is size-picked several times when the price is optimum. The trees are finally "stripped" in late June to mid August, again depending on price. Timing is a guessing game because price fluctuations are unpredictably defined by market demand.

Fortunately the maturing grove has lived up to our expectations of fully paying for itself and producing enough income to pay for our property taxes and annual insurance premiums.

In my opinion, a good retirement should be a balance between mental, physical and social activities. Bridge provides the mental challenges; the grove and gym provide enough physical workouts and family and friends provide the needed social stimulation.

My vision of family "Sunday dinner" has turned into a reality. Barbara and I cook dinner every Sunday and everyone comes. Dinner could be anything from a full-blown homemade spaghetti dinner to simple sandwiches and salad. We often have time to play active games of Wii, Gestures, Family Feud or Trivial Pursuit. We are competitive and all enjoy the "bonding" time. Sometimes, everyone is busy with other activities, so they drop by, eat and run. This is all right with us because we have a chance to see them every week.

The vacation tradition with friends is still ongoing with annual vacations consisting of tours or cruises to different parts of the world. These have been entertaining and, more importantly, re-enforce the idea that we are very fortunate to live in the USA. Regardless of how bad we may perceive our government to be, it is far better than many around the world.

I am almost "vacationed out" however. I have seen many churches, museums and different cultures so my lust for adventure is essentially satisfied. I'm thankful that we had the opportunity to experience these while we are healthy and able.

Barbara and I are very fortunate to have a full, active, and enjoyable life. As everyone else, we encountered a few bumps but as we look back, the good far outweighs the bad. Our most treasured memories are centered on our very close relationships with our families and friends.

We have lived and continue to live a full life. Our successes have contributed to our confidence and well being and our failures have kept us grounded. We are privileged to have accomplished everything we set out to do and are now living in Utopia.

The End

Epilogue

At this snippet in time (Jan, 2011), all three children and their families are happy, healthy and surviving the biggest recession of our times.

Dianne and Dale Tattersall live a few minutes away from our house. Dianne got her real estate license and is extremely busy negotiating the world of bank foreclosures, repossessions and short sales. Dale is a busy Sempra executive dealing with upgrading military bases to new clean energy systems. Dale and Dianne are on the verge of having three daughters in college simultaneously. Tara is in her junior year at Fresno State University and she is active in many school activities. Alexa and Jenna are about to finish high school. Both excel scholastically and in soccer and hope to be rewarded with scholastic and/or sports scholarships. Barbara and I accompanied them to visit some east coast colleges. We visited the University of Rochester, Cornell, RPI, Boston University, Harvard, Yale, NYU and Columbia. Alexa, the high school senior, is leaning towards attending USC, followed by attending the UCLA medical school, and Jenna has her heart set at Yale. I hope she makes it!!

Jessica and Shawn Macdonald also live a few minutes away. Jessica is a high school World History teacher. She loves her challenging job and was promoted to department head her second year of teaching. Shawn was a small business administration (SBA) bank executive, but is taking a few months off to be a house dad to care for their two young children, cook and keep house. He is doing a great job and Jess loves it. Their daughter Mia is a smart, dynamic six year old, full of wonder and excitement. Her brother Max is a 23-month-old bundle of joy. He is good looking with lots of blond curls and blue eyes and will probably grow up to be a heart breaker. Max's personality is emerging as a joker and big tease. He laughs easily and is very accommodating. Finally someone is taking after his grandfather.

Matthew found and married his soul-mate Glance last year. She is a wonderful girl from the Philippines. Poor Glance had to put up with our family's scrutiny from the moment we met her. We warned Matt to prepare her to answer a question from each of us during her first visit. She agreed and came prepared with her own set of questions for us, which broke the ice. We loved her the moment we met her and she quickly adapted to our idiosyncrasies. Matt and Glance live in Valencia, CA. Matt is a sound engineer who specializes in restoring and conforming motion picture film sound tracks. Glance has a business degree but is temporarily working as a home caregiver. She just brought her three-year-old son, Justin, from the Philippines and is expecting a new baby girl in May 2011. Matthew, the empathetic one, turned out to be a great father and all are doing well. Our newest grandchildren, Justin and his baby sister are destined to continue in the Mina tradition of good looks, intelligence and more importantly, total humility.

Top row left to right: Matt, Glance, Dianne, Dale and Shawn. Bottom row: Mia, Barbara, Justin, Jenna, Tara, Alexa, Jessica, myself and Max

Acknowledgements

My family and I are grateful to my friend and ex brother-in-law Dan McManus who planted the idea of writing my life story. The idea sprouted into reality and he continued to show an interest by taking the time to review, edit and remove the many superfluous commas I tended to include.

I also want to thank my friend Charlie Hurd, who enthusiastically read each segment as it was completed and provided me with constant encouragement and feedback.

Finally, I must extend my appreciation to my daughter, Jessica Macdonald, for thoughtfully digesting the manuscript and reminding me to include many forgotten episodes. I also want to thank Barbara for painstakingly correcting my grammatical and spelling errors and my friend Bob Gibbons for his glowing introduction.

Last but not least, I am completely indebted to my sister-in-law, Susan Ross, for her final review and valuable improvements. She read the manuscript several times and suggested many content and sentence structure changes. She helped me polish this book to its final form.

Thank you!

Appendix

I have been attracted to cars since early childhood and think that a person's car reflects his or her personality. I thought it would be fun to show you the cars I have owned and let you be the judge. All the cars listed are the same models as mine. I did not bother to list my company cars, which should have no correlation with my personality.

1959 Opel Rekord

1963 Plymouth Valiant - nerd time

1955 Chevrolet Bel Air convertible

1962 Pontiac Tempest Le Mans

1966 Volkswagen

1962 MG Midget

1959 Rambler – Seats reclined

1967 Dodge Dart Convertible

1969 Volkswagen

1973 Ford Pinto wagon

1974 BMW 2002 - My favorite

1997 Jeep Grand Cherokee

1999 Lexus Rx300

2002 Mini Cooper

2002 Honda Shadow Spirit VT 750

2005 Toyota Tundra

6413993R00112

Made in the USA
San Bernardino, CA
08 December 2013